ADVANCE

"*One Life* hits the epicentre of what we are fighting for every single day in Joe & The Juice. Namely, to build a brand that delivers an unseen level of meaningfulness in the intersection between our people and our workplace. This is a must read for anyone who is ambitious about life."

Kaspar Basse, Founder and Executive Chairman, Joe & The Juice

"Leadership is about creating 'movement' on two dimensions – continuously setting the right coordinates for the direction and making sure each and every employee feels a genuine meaning in what they do. Morten's book should be read by every leader or aspiring professional."

Stine Bosse, Director of the Supervisory Board, Allianz Group and appointed as one of the most influential businesswomen in the world by the *Financial Times*

"Morten delivers an inconvenient but extremely enlightening critique of humanity while providing optimistic answers to how we can navigate our lives, our businesses and our society towards a better and more sustainable future. All organizations should indeed define and work for a higher purpose than just profit, so this book should be an embedded part of all leadership curricula."

Professor Flemming Besenbacher, Chairman, Carlsberg Group and the Carlsberg Foundation

Published by
LID Publishing Limited
The Record Hall, Studio 204,
16-16a Baldwins Gardens,
London EC1N 7RJ, UK

info@lidpublishing.com
www.lidpublishing.com

A member of:

businesspublishersroundtable.com

Printed in Latvia by Jelgavas Tipogrāfija
ISBN: 978-1-912555-59-8

Originally published in Denmark as:
Ét liv Én tid Ét menneske
Gyldendal A/S (2018)

Translation: Tam McTurk, Citadel Translations
Cover and page design: Matthew Renaudin

ONE LIFE

HOW WE FORGOT TO LIVE MEANINGFUL LIVES

MORTEN ALBÆK

MADRID | MEXICO CITY | LONDON
NEW YORK | BUENOS AIRES
BOGOTA | SHANGHAI | NEW DELHI

CONTENTS

PREFACE   1

INTRODUCTION.   9
THE GREAT PARADOX

The happiness enigma

The working person

The difference between satisfaction,
happiness and meaningfulness

CHAPTER 1.   22
ONE LIFE, IN ONE TIME,
AS ONE HUMAN BEING

The three semantic manipulations

Speed is the new god

CHAPTER 2.   42
THE LADDER OF SELF-RESPECT

Self-insight creates self-awareness

Self-awareness creates self-worth

Self-worth creates self-respect

The existential immune system

CHAPTER 3.   64
INHUMAN MANAGEMENT

Work-life (im)balance

Leave me in peace

Dearth of morality

Leadership as a mutual existential demand

CHAPTER 4.   82
PROFESSIONAL INTIMACY
AND PLATONIC LOVE

Professional distance

Apollo and Dionysus

Why you should love your boss – and vice versa

CHAPTER 5.   96
MEANINGFUL LEADERSHIP

IQ vs EQ vs MQ

Meaningfulness Quotient (MQ)

Performance management 2.0: The MQ analysis

From Human Resource Management to Human
Potential Leadership

Flexibility at work is the key, not balance between life and work

The meaningfulness conversation

CHAPTER 6.   **124**
HUMANISTIC CAPITALISM

CHAPTER 7.   **132**
LOYALTY AND MUTINY

The difference between values and virtues

Self-awareness as a means to understanding
your purpose and virtues

Mutiny – how far should you go as an individual?

How far should an organization go to defend its purpose?

CHAPTER 8.   **148**
HOW FAR SHOULD WE GO AS A SOCIETY?

From GDP to happiness index to meaningfulness index

EPILOGUE   **156**

ACKNOWLEDGMENTS   **161**

ENDNOTES   **163**

PREFACE

On 19 July 2008, my brothers, nephew and I jumped into my older brother's Citroën Berlingo and raced 260 miles north from Copenhagen to Aalborg Hospital. One of the nurses looking after my father had called to say that he could breathe his last at any moment. We made it to the hospital late in the evening and half walked, half ran to his room, a bit breathless. Mum was standing at his bedside, looking remarkably composed. Dad sat propped up in the hospital bed. His normally full face was hollowed out, the greyish-yellow skin stretched so tautly that his cheekbones looked like they might pop through at any moment.

He welcomed us in a surprisingly clear and vigorous voice. "Did you really think things were so bad that you all had to rush here in the middle of the night?"

"Yes, Dad, we did," I replied.

"Well, you're wrong – again!" he responded.

We all laughed. Loudly. It was lovely. But when the laughter subsided, it was replaced with silence. We looked at each other. At him. Our father, grandfather and husband. "We've done all right together, haven't we?," he asked, and answered himself. "Well, I think so anyway."

I felt a lump in my throat; I had difficulty breathing. Tears began to trickle down my cheeks. "Yes, Dad, we have," we replied.

"We've made so many good memories together," he added. Then, turning to one of my brothers, he said, "I know you've sometimes doubted that I love you, but I do. I always have."

"I know, Dad," my brother replied.

At that moment, my heart felt as if it was bursting – but also being transformed – and my mind was flooded with a blend of sorrow and relief. Sorrow that any minute now my mother would be a widow and my brothers and I would lose our dad. Relief that we were all there together, sharing this final fond farewell. Dad turned to me and said, "Morten, can you say something funny? We could all do with a laugh." Soon afterward, we kissed him goodbye. He closed his tired eyes and fell asleep, never to wake. My father, Ole Albæk, died on 20 July 2008 at the age of 64.

Dad was buried on 26 July in our local cemetery in the far rural north of Jutland. It was a warm, sunny day. Not a pew was empty, and people had to stand in and around the doorway, straining to hear the organ, the first psalm, the minister's prayer, the reading from the Gospel of John and the eulogy that I delivered on behalf of myself and my brothers. I stood in front of the coffin, flanked by my brothers. "Dear Dad, you were no ordinary father," I began. "You were an extraordinary father. A very special one. You were our dad. And we loved you very dearly." I looked up, scanning the packed church, recognizing one tear-stained face after the other. But I stopped abruptly as my eyes met the puzzled faces of my two small children. Suddenly aware that one day they would be standing in my shoes, bidding farewell to me – their father – my voice cracked.

Memories of Dad's death and funeral have stayed with me ever since. The ceremony in the Church, and the events in the days, weeks, months and years that followed, afforded me one particular, vital insight into life – the meaning of which I didn't fully comprehend at first. Perhaps I was too young, immature and inexperienced to understand it back then, but I gradually came to the realization that there is a fundamental and important difference between feeling satisfaction, happiness and a sense of meaning in life. Satisfaction was the last thing I felt right then. Happiness was the furthest emotion from my mind. But in there somewhere, amid the grief, loss and tears, an unmistakable sense of meaningfulness surged through my body and mind. A sense of gratitude. A sense of dignity and hope. Even a real zest for and appreciation of life.

Ever since that summer day, more than a decade ago, I have been unable to shake the thought that in our culture, upbringing and education, we have completely lost sight of the difference between satisfaction, happiness and meaning. Years of studying this issue in depth has made me even more convinced that our failure to distinguish between these three states of mind is one of the main reasons that so many of us lose our way and are unable to lead ourselves or others to the kind of life to which we undoubtedly have the potential – a life endowed with good mental health and existential quality.

This book is about showing that nothing is more important than living a life that is meaningful – not just one that is fleetingly satisfactory or happy.

On a routine flight from Portland, Oregon to New York four years after my father's funeral, I read something that truly changed my way of thinking. It was a typical domestic flight – the banal rituals of mass transit, full of artificial smiles and forced proximity – but I remember with spine-tingling clarity reading a short, semi-scientific article that transformed the sterile fuselage into the setting for what would turn out, a few months later, to be a defining moment in my life, as both a human being and a business executive. An Australian hospice nurse had spent years documenting conversations with people for whom the next month, week, day or breath could be their last. Irrespective of class, financial status, ethnicity and sexuality, no matter whether they were fat or thin, tall or short, married or single, black or white, they shared five fundamental regrets about their lives:[1]

1. They regretted not keeping in touch with their friends
2. They regretted not having allowed themselves to be happier
3. They regretted not having had the courage to express their feelings more
4. They regretted not having the courage to live a life truer to themselves, rather than the life others expected of them
5. They regretted spending so much of their lives at work

As somebody involved in the higher echelons of the business world at the time, it was the fifth regret that had the greatest effect on me and triggered a sharp existential intake of breath.

The uneasy feeling lasted for several months, until I decided to take all of the advice and experiences I had eagerly absorbed and paid for dearly over many years in the business world and throw them out the window – out into the infinite universe of indifference. All the well-intentioned advice passed on by professional, gifted, hard-working and amiable managers, colleagues, consultants and professors at world-renowned management institutions amounts to nothing if we end up regretting the time that we spent working or training for it. From that day forth, I swore that nobody under my leadership would ever look back on that period of their life with regret.

My focus was to ensure that work makes life meaningful. This is far from easy, I hasten to add, and let me be the first to say that I am not sure how well I have succeeded. In business, managers have the privilege and responsibility, directly and indirectly, via their position and leadership, to influence the lives of hundreds or even thousands of people. But as you climb the hierarchy, you are force-fed a standard diet of thin, misguided management literature. You simply cannot avoid the kind of modern management lingo that doggedly tries to make you forget that your staff are, above all else, human beings, each of whom has the potential to make the one life they live as meaningful as possible.

So, how do we turn things around? How do we make sure that future generations in hospices look back on their 'working lives' as something that enriched their lives as a whole, by imbuing it with the meaning and quality that they deserve? As I tried to answer these questions, it became clear to me, slowly but surely, that the only way to do so is by challenging – even attacking and dismantling – the artificial language that surrounds us. I realized that the path to a life with as few regrets and as much meaning as possible requires confronting what I call the three great semantic manipulations: the way in which our everyday language attempts to split life, time and, ultimately, the individual human being. Does it really make any sense to talk about *work life* as something different from *private life*? Do we not only have one life? And if we do have just one life, in one time, time that passes and never comes back again, does it make any sense to insist on splitting it, in the language we use, into *work time, leisure time* and *family time*? Isn't it all just time? And if we do just have one life, lived in time that will never return, does it make any sense to insist upon dividing ourselves linguistically into three people: one who works, one who plays, and one who spends time with family or on other leisure pursuits? After all, we are born as one person and die as one person. My father only had one funeral, and there was only one coffin in the church.

The Australian nurse had inspired me to realize that phrases like work-life balance, which imply that the two are different, are ultimately meaningless. Each of us lives one big, complex life. Regardless of how and when that life ends, we all want to live it as meaningfully as possible.

I want to encourage reflection on the paradox that affects us all – that prosperity no longer translates into existential wellbeing, a concept far more all-embracing than just a high standard of living. Existential wellbeing implies a high quality of life in all of its most fundamental aspects. It covers everything relating to or affirming our existence, the very essence of our being. We have never been wealthier, lived longer, been so well educated or so interconnected via technology. Yet meaninglessness is taking up permanent residence in more and more of us, especially in people who work, as well as young people. We have never been as medicated, lonely, stressed, anxious and depressed as we are right now.

Merely acknowledging the paradox is not enough. Something has to be done about it. One in eight people in Denmark now suffers from mental health problems.[2] Extrapolating on this trend, by the time my daughter enters the world of work a decade from now, one in five of her compatriots will suffer from poor mental health. As they embark on their working lives, my children are much more likely than any generation before them to suffer from stress-related and mental health issues. And this is not characteristic only of Danish adolescents. Whether you are a teenager in Beijing, London or San Francisco, the prospects are similar.

Any such projection invariably entails a multitude of unknown factors and uncertain assumptions, of course, but it is an alarming trend nevertheless, and one that shows no sign of slowing down unless we start to do things in a radically different way. We need to start by teaching ourselves and the generations to come the art of living a meaningful life, an existential art that appears to have been forgotten or to have fallen out of fashion and is, at the very least, in need of an in-depth revision.

I am well aware that I am neither the world's greatest leader nor its greatest philosopher, and never will be. However, over nearly two decades, I have had the privilege of spending time in what I like to call a 'living philosophical laboratory'. As both an employee and a guinea pig, I have had first-hand experience of meaningless management. Later, as a leader and 'laboratory technician', I experimented tirelessly in the hope of finding an antidote. As an honorary professor and international executive, I have walked the fine line between humanism and capitalism, and in my eagerness have undoubtedly stepped on toes on both sides of it. I make no claim to have seen a burning bush or discovered the philosopher's stone, but I have beheld both capitalism and humanism from various angles. As a human being, employee, entrepreneur, employer and philosopher, I have attempted to reconcile the two.

This book opens my 'laboratory' up to the world, shares my experiences and sets out some of the ideas and concepts that I have developed and applied in an attempt to find 'meaning in the madness' in my one life. In all relationships, I believe that every conversation should start and end with the question of what constitutes a good life. This question is applicable to everyone, no matter whether they are a young person on the cusp of adult life, a veteran teacher, a parent of four, or a boss responsible for thousands of people.

For me, a good life is a meaningful one. This book is about how we have lost sight of that fact. This to me is absurd, as meaning is proven to be the most important basic ingredient for the sustainability of our lives, our businesses and our society.

I am grateful that you have chosen to devote some of your time in your one life to read what I have to say.

Morten Albæk
Denmark, 2019

INTRODUCTION
THE GREAT PARADOX

The average newborn has a better starting point in life now than ever before. You might not think so, given the unrelenting negativity of newspaper headlines and the apocalyptic nature of TV reporting, but civilization is actually making excellent progress. So much so, in fact, that the World Economic Forum[3] proclaimed the world a better place than ever, adding that the outlook for the future was positive in every possible way. In a recent speech, Barack Obama asserted that if you could choose one point in history at which to be born, then it would be right now. It would be sheer folly to try to understand the world via tabloid journalism. Crises break out suddenly and violently, whereas prosperity, health and education all improve gradually over time.

Measured in terms of external indicators, and seen from a bird's eye perspective, we have become better off in every conceivable way as economic and technological quantum leaps have driven the world forward. We live longer, enjoy greater prosperity, are better educated, have more opportunities and are more interconnected than ever before. In short, it has never been easier to live a better life. The question is whether the prospect of a longer, more prosperous, more enlightened and more interconnected life than ever before has actually made us better at living life. Has progress improved our existential wellbeing?

These were precisely the type of questions that the UN set out to answer in 2012 when the Secretary-General, Ban Ki-moon, set up the UN Sustainable Development Solutions Network. One of its key aims was to map global happiness. Since then, the UN has published an annual 'World Happiness Report', which covers more than 150 countries. The rankings are based on data gathered by Gallup. Since 2005, Gallup has been conducting national studies of how countries perform in terms of their economy, social security, health, freedom, generosity and corruption – the very factors that, according to the report, have the greatest overall impact on an individual's sense of happiness. The top spot alternates between a trio of the Nordic countries, Finland, Norway and Denmark, which are almost three times happier than the lowest-ranked country, South Sudan.

Despite topping the rankings for happiness and other indicators of progress, many affluent countries, including my home country Denmark, have also become a lot more prosperous in recent decades, but not much happier in the statistics, and sometimes even less happy. The phenomenon of being better off but less happy is, unfortunately, a syndrome in many parts of the world. And it isn't just a matter of wealth not automatically translating into wellbeing – never before in history have we been more depressed, anxious, medicated and lonely than we are today.

According to a 2019 report, *Global Happiness and Wellbeing*, the burden of mental illness accounts for between 7% and 13% of disability-adjusted life years worldwide.[4] The World Health Organization (WHO) estimates that more than 300 million people suffer from depression. In terms of the numbers of years spent living with the condition, depression represents the biggest global health crisis. It is on the rise, and the trend looks set to continue.[5] The WHO anticipates that depression will be the biggest contributor to the overall global burden of disease by 2030.[6] The number of people suffering from anxiety is also on the rise.[7] In the United States, it is estimated that 28% of the population feels lonely, while loneliness in the United Kingdom is considered such a serious problem that a national 'Campaign to End Loneliness' has been launched.[8]

We must of course always be careful not to rely too heavily on averages and generalizations. But there is no getting away from it: mental illness has never been so widespread and severe.

In other words, we face a remarkable schism. The majority of us have everything we need to live a good life, but many of us feel frankly awful. In other words, we lack the existential equilibrium needed to translate all the wealth and welfare of our world into life quality and wellbeing.

THE HAPPINESS ENIGMA

It is often said that the answer you receive depends on the question you ask. We could spend from here to eternity discussing what the UN happiness indicators actually measure. Are we really as happy as the study shows? Does the way the UN uses the concept carry any philosophical weight at all? Does it make any sense to speak of a happy people if happiness is nothing but a fleeting moment in an individual's life?

In sociology, the Thomas theorem says that, "If men define situations as real, they are real in their consequences." In other words, the outcome of a situation depends on our perception of it, not on the situation *per se*. When my children were small and afraid of the monster under their bed, it was pretty imma- terial whether or not the monster actually existed. For them, the situation was real and so were the consequences. Children will continue to be afraid of what they think is under the bed and beg their parents to leave the light on. Transposed to the discussion about happiness, what is crucial is not external factors. The only thing that is crucial is that happiness is real when we feel happy. In the Nordic countries, if we keep telling ourselves that we live in some of the happiest countries in the world, we will end up believing it, regardless of whether the emperor is wearing any clothes or not.

Denmark is a prime example. First, we rank among the global socio-economic elite in terms of both our standard of living and how happy we feel. Just as there has never been a better time to be born into the world, there are few better places to be born than Denmark. Second, boasting about our happiness and derivative terms such as 'hygge' has become our signature trait, to such an extent that nobody is left in any doubt that it is a better society than any other and that life in Denmark is *unbelievably* good.

We like to tell ourselves – and anybody else who will listen – that this happiness is entirely of our own making. Ultimately, Denmark's most important raw material is knowledge, and we have only ourselves to thank for our democratic values and our ability to work with each other. We believe that this gives Denmark a self-generated and self-sustainable advantage in a competitive, globalised economy. Nor are we shy about marketing ourselves as the happiest country in the world. And why shouldn't we? After all, it would be hard to tempt tourists or attract labour to a nation of miserable people crushed by despondency. But just how well dressed is the emperor?

When we compare our ranking as one of the happiest countries in the world with our levels of stress, depression and anxiety, it's clear that the Danish case is also a prime example of how wealth does not translate directly into wellbeing or happiness. In fact, the Danish fairy tale has become a tragedy. More than 6% of the population suffer from severe loneliness, approximately one in five experience stress in their daily life, while the number of young people living with depression has tripled since the turn of the millennium.[9] Despite the unimaginably positive socio-economic conditions and the greatest possible belief in our own state of bliss, our mental health has suffered.

THE WORKING PERSON

According to German sociologist and economist Max Weber, the rise of capitalism was inextricably linked to Protestantism, which elevated work to a calling, and a moderate and active life to the means by which the faithful achieved eternal salvation. This concept of hard work in the hope of a blissful afterlife helped lay the foundation for capitalism. Since the relationship between faith and the economy has been discussed in detail elsewhere, it will suffice for the purposes of this book to say that it is reasonable to assert that work has a special role and value in the Western world.

"Hard work is its own reward" may be an old saying, but the basic point is still very much alive and kicking. We often hear people who have been made unemployed say things like, "All of a sudden, I had nothing to get up for." Work truly does have an indisputable value in our society – a value so great that our identity is tied up with it. When we meet someone for the first time, we are often asked, "Who are you?" And we answer – often without hesitation – by telling them what our job is and even term work as "what we do for a living".

Little wonder, then, that work should be such a source of stress, depression and anxiety. It is even tempting to conclude that it more closely resembles the path to damnation than to salvation.

According to Gallup's latest "State of the Global Workplace" study, 85% of the global workforce are unengaged with their work,[10] costing the economy an estimated USD 7,000 billion p.a. in lost productivity.[11] According to the Mental Health Foundation, 74% of people have at some point felt so stressed that they were overwhelmed or unable to cope.[12] Although we are surrounded by colleagues and spend most of our waking hours in their company, we do not necessarily have strong social ties at work. One large-scale study indicated that slightly more than half feel lonely always or very often at work.[13] In other words, we feel bad in our lives largely because we feel bad in our work. The main effect of our good living conditions, increased prosperity or perceived happiness is that it causes us to collectively recite the mantra that we have never been freer, better off, more educated or lived for so long – and we accept this as a proxy for greater wellbeing.

Perhaps this also explains the widespread mental health problems in recent years. No matter how loudly we intone the mantra, and how much we repeat the indicators of apparent progress, we cannot escape reality. The body and the mind are astute, and neither pays any heed to our flights of fancy.

As the Danish philosopher Villy Sørensen so aptly put it in 1971:

> That increasing prosperity should lead to increasing dissatisfaction seems unreasonable, because the causes of dissatisfaction should be fewer; but, reasonably enough, any (social) activity that is not immediately driven by need must have a purpose. As this development also entails tendencies toward the depersonalization of social relations, the need of the individual to find meaning in it all becomes all the more powerful.[14]

Almost half a century ago, Sørensen was emphasizing that there isn't necessarily a 1:1 correlation between prosperity and a sense of meaning. In other words, we cannot expect that improving our ability to generate wealth will automatically improve our ability to find meaning in life.

The prevalence of stress, anxiety and depression in affluent parts of the world undeniably makes our experience of progress appear to be something of a sham, if not downright bogus. The extent of work's contribution to social problems raises an obvious question: why on Earth is it not taken more seriously that the activity that occupies us for (on average) more than half of our waking hours makes so many of us ill? How absolutely ridiculous does that make us look? We're living longer than ever, but our reaction to that is to work ourselves half to death and regret it when reminded of our mortality. This is not necessarily physical, but in the sense that we allow the form and content of our work to cause us such severe human problems that, either directly or via their effect on our health, they seriously diminish our ability to live a good life.

Work poses many and varied challenges. Self-help gurus and life coaches offer one kind of answer to them, politicians and interest groups another, and doctors, psychologists and sociologists yet another.

My point with this book is quite different – to offer what I hope is a useful and practical philosophical answer to a problem that is ultimately existential, because it concerns our relationship with ourselves and the whole of the one life we have been given. First, I want to challenge the view that appears to be common among most of the contributors to this debate, namely, that the explanation for work making us ill is to be found in the blurring of the boundaries between our so-called working and nonworking lives. I also want to tackle the idea that the solution lies in separating the two. I utterly reject the premise of both the diagnosis and the solution: that it is possible to compartmentalize our lives neatly in this way. I'm well aware that it is controversial to wipe out any distinction between the time that we spend at work and the time that we spend on everything else. I also understand that for some, this may sound like the shortest path to wreaking even greater havoc upon human life and potential. However, we have spent decades conducting millions of employee reviews and appraisals and preaching the sermon of work-life balance so fervently that it has been elevated almost to the status of a religion. And yet, at the same time, and despite our best intentions, we cannot help but conclude that people are becoming more and more ill as a result of their work. I do not think that more of the same is the solution to the great existential challenge that we – as parents, friends, romantic partners, employees, managers, shareholders, politicians or citizens – need to confront.

Against this backdrop, I offer my suggestion as to how we, as the single individuals we are, can each embrace the opportunities that our world provides, including in the workplace, and transform them into existential rewards by using *meaningfulness* as a currency.

THE DIFFERENCE BETWEEN SATISFACTION, HAPPINESS AND MEANINGFULNESS

Why meaningfulness as a currency rather than satisfaction or happiness? Well, the first and most straightforward answer is that the last two can be ruled out. If they were the ultimate goals of civilization, and they worked, then the existential carnage being wreaked at the moment would, quite simply, not be happening. But many of us *are* suffering from existential malnutrition as things stand, despite us having every reason to be satisfied and happy in purely material terms. Deciphering what exactly the three concepts mean might be a good place to start our quest to explain why we should choose meaningfulness as our currency.

Satisfaction is the meeting of a need. If I meet my needs, I am satisfied. You have an expectation of something, and the realization of it triggers a sense of satisfaction. For instance, if I want an apple, I get an apple and I'm satisfied. Or, if my son wants ice cream, he gets ice cream and he's satisfied – at least until he is finished and immediately wants another. This phenomenon leads those in management to attempt to satisfy their employees by offering them benefits such as fresh fruit, dry-cleaning services, in-service training and even higher pay. Fringe benefits may well make it easier to tolerate going to work, but it would be something of a stretch to claim that they instil a strong sense of joy in life. Satisfaction may provide a decent starting point, but it is quite simply not enough to want to live a life primarily based on it.

Happiness is the experience of everything coming together beautifully in the moment. It's a form of existential orgasm, with glitter and confetti exploding all around, rendering us euphoric about the fact that life offers a moment of unbridled enthusiasm, in which we feel, temporarily, as if we can defy the laws of gravity. But it's only a moment, whether it's the first rush of new love, seeing your team score the winning goal in the very last second, or seeing someone you've missed badly. In that moment, the inner tension between idea and execution, between reality and dream, is momentarily blurred. It is a euphoric, but ephemeral, climax. The experience of happiness is the opposite of the everyday, the humdrum. Happiness is by nature extraordinary, which makes it impossible to be happy all of the time. And semantically, if the extraordinary were everyday life, then it would be simply ordinary. Some manage it more often than others, but nobody is happy all of the time. It is a cruel paradox that a life lived in the pursuit of happiness and passing pleasure will lead, at worst, to the very opposite – loneliness, emptiness, unhappiness. If the pursuit of short-lived happiness were indeed the highest goal in life, we would be prepared to disregard anything that stood in the way of achieving it. We would constantly forsake partners, friends and jobs in pursuit of ever greater pleasures just around the next corner. And we would almost certainly end up lonely and unhappy. It is unrealistic to want a life filled mainly with happiness, and pursuing it constantly is an unsustainable strategy for life.

Meaningfulness is not about realizing a need, or about a short-lived burst of joy. Meaning is the feeling that your life has dignity and hope, that forearmed with all of the knowledge accumulated throughout your life, you are able to look backward, sideways and forward with self-worth and self-respect. It is a meaning that comes from belonging, from having a higher purpose and from feeling that you are either already – or at least are on the way to – the right place for you in life.

However, meaning doesn't emerge from thin air. It is created. And maintaining it is hard work because meaningfulness is constantly put to the test. The initial euphoria of falling in love is followed by the hard work of keeping the relationship alive. The goal in the very last second is preceded by multiple missed chances. The reunion with a loved one follows days, weeks or months of yearning. Meaningfulness is created not in moments of delirious intoxication. It is the sum total of the experiences of what is right for us on our personal balance sheets.

Meaningfulness accommodates aspects of life that are not necessarily bright and positive. Grief, for example, is incompatible with satisfaction. It is an unsatisfactory emotion. You can't be happy and grieving at the same time. But you *can* feel grief and a sense of meaning at the same time. Few people would say that burying a loved one was satisfying. Fewer still would claim that it brought them happiness. But many of us find the occasion extremely meaningful. It reminds us what brought us closer to the person we loved and provides perspective on our own future.

We can't be brimming with joy and happiness all of the time. I would also contend that joy and being joyful are more akin to satisfaction and happiness than to meaning. The same applies to joy as to happiness and, for that matter, to satisfaction. You can't go around jumping with joy all the time, because sometimes there will be things to be sad about. Nor can you go around being satisfied all the time, because sometimes there will be things to be dissatisfied with. But you *can* still find a sense of meaning in your life, no matter whether you are satisfied or dissatisfied, happy or sad.

We have learned to keep our misery and mediocrity, our dissatisfaction and unhappiness, to ourselves. All of us contribute to a form of collective self-deception, telling ourselves and others that we are all constantly conquering ever higher peaks, even though this is rarely the case. "How are you?" we ask each other in passing. "Fine," we respond. We never contemplate an honest answer, let alone daring to give one for fear of the social consequences. If one day we finally mustered up the courage to answer honestly and share the full extent of our misery, all but a few would see our honesty as a nuisance rather than a gift. Who has the time to listen to that?

We know these themes from classical philosophy. Aristotle offers a perspective that stands in contrast to the notion of happiness as something deriving from lust or pleasure, as a moment of ecstasy. For Aristotle, happiness *is* the goal, but it is not the content of a life that determines whether it is a happy one or not. Rather, happiness is determined primarily by the way in which a person relates to that content. In this view, we all start at zero and are equal. It is not about wealth, education or status, but ethics and virtues. For Aristotle, happiness is independent of good fortune or ill fortune. It is about the ethical virtues to which you adhere throughout life's ups and downs, and the discipline with which you do so. He contends that even when life is anything but positive and bright, it can still be happy. Conversely, a life full of good fortune and light can still be unhappy.

Aristotle's concept of happiness or the highest good – *eudaimonia* – is far closer to meaningfulness than to our modern idea of happiness. In fact, it is perfectly legitimate to question whether the UN's happiness indicators really quantify happiness. Given that they are based primarily on socio-economic indicators, such as GDP, social security, health, freedom, generosity and corruption, are they not simply a measurement of satisfaction? Certainly, if you asked Aristotle, he would say that, apart from perhaps generosity, such factors have nothing to do with happiness. And if you asked me, I'd say that they have nothing to do with meaningfulness. On the contrary, they describe the circumstances in which we live. They say nothing about how we respond to the fluctuations in our lives, whether upward, downward or, more commonly, sideways.

In other words, we have messed about with the definition of happiness to such an extent that it is now more about winning the lottery than about seeking a meaningful existence. It is precisely for that reason that we must clearly distinguish between satisfaction, happiness and meaning as we move forward in the 21st century.

1

ONE LIFE,
IN ONE TIME,
AS ONE HUMAN BEING

Saint Augustine wrote in his *Confessions* around 400 AD, "What then is time? If no one asks me, I know what it is. If I wish to explain it to him who asks, I do not know."[15] You might think that we've learned a bit more since then, but perhaps we have not.

THE THREE SEMANTIC MANIPULATIONS

While it is true that ethics and profit are not mutually exclusive by definition, it is equally true that the quest for profit has often had gravely unethical consequences. The tail end of the 2000s saw the worst financial crisis since the Great Depression of the 1920s and 1930s. Iconic banking giants toppled like dominoes, leaving in their wake a gaping economic vacuum. When the dust had settled and someone had to clean up the mess, the initial shock quickly transformed into a moral vendetta. How could this tiny, well-to-do banking elite get away with gambling so recklessly – not to mention losing – on the financial markets? What drove these self-styled supermen in pin-striped suits to pursue such unfettered greed? After all, beneath all the bluster and bravado, they are mere mortals like the rest of us.

While researching this question, two professors, Mats Alvesson and Maxine Robertson, made some interesting findings.[16] By studying a handful of well-established investment bankers in Britain, they improved their understanding of how money affects identity. In every single case, when the bankers were confronted with choices or circumstances that were at odds with their own identity or moral compass, they invariably used material resources (money) to rationalize and justify their decisions. Even though they were in no doubt about the dubious ethics or downright immorality of their actions, the magnitude of the material returns they stood to gain by ignoring morality and identity encouraged them to keep going. Alvesson and Robertson call this syndrome 'Teflonic Identity Manoeuvring'. We are all familiar with Teflon, a material used to make frying pans nonstick. And we are also familiar with the concept of manoeuvring when learning to drive, specifically, how to safely navigate a car around obstacles or in adverse conditions. These experienced investment bankers had essentially coated their identity with a layer of Teflon to ensure that decisions made at work didn't stick to them. This allowed them to navigate their identity through the moral dilemmas thrown up by their work without any scratches on their surface.

In effect, they split their identity in two: one persona at work, another in private. This detachment enabled them to circumvent any deeper personal meaning in their work; it simply did not exist for them. Their work may have been meaningless, but they believed a high enough yield compensated for that fact. But does this only apply to investment bankers? What about the rest of us? Are we also Teflon-coated, or do we manage to retain our identity and moral compass in all facets of our lives?

We like to tell ourselves and each other that life is infinitely bigger and more beautiful than just the hours totted up on our payslips. We like to think that we're so much more than our work and that we can't be reduced to the titles on our name badges and e-mail signatures. However, when asked who we are, the majority of us respond, intuitively and without hesitation, with our profession and title. If the first statement above were true – that our lives and identities are simply too big and too beautiful to be captured simply by what our job is – then we should just as intuitively and unhesitatingly respond that we are a father or mother, husband or wife, a friend or a lover, a brother or a sister. But we don't. We learn early on that professional labels have a higher value, an assertion that few if any of us ever really challenge.

Those privileged enough to have jobs spend around eight out of every 24 hours sleeping, eight working and eight on everything else. In other words, around half of our waking hours are devoted to being available to the labour market and the other half is spent on all our other roles and titles in life.

But we are all just one person. When I get up in the morning and look in the mirror, I reach the same conclusion every time: that there is only one Morten looking back at me, despite my many different titles. We live only one life, in one time, which flies by at an incredible speed, despite our many activities. One challenge presented by time is that it is so close to us that we can't really relate to it. As a result, we often subconsciously manage our time without giving any thought to the fact that it is disappearing forever. If we manage time badly, we manage life badly because our lives are ultimately no more than the sum of the time between our first and last heartbeats.

The German philosopher Martin Heidegger devoted most of his waking hours to trying to understand how it is possible that the things that are the closest to us are also the things about which we know the least. A good example is our relationship with time. It is interesting to think about how often we say, write or hear the word 'time', despite not having much understanding of what it actually is. Heidegger's theory is that when something is that close to us, it is almost as if it is blurred.

Toward the end of the 17th century, Isaac Newton proved that time is absolute and universal. In other words, time exists independently of any event or human experience. If the universe were completely devoid of existence and content, time would continue regardless. In the early 20th century, Albert Einstein's Theory of Relativity expanded this understanding, but Newton's theory of time remains valid for anything that does not move at the speed of light or faster, and for anything not significantly affected by extremes of gravity. Unless we plan to move at the speed of light (which might make it difficult to enjoy the moment) or become astronauts and allow ourselves to be sucked into a black hole, we must accept that time is absolute. We can't stop time. Nor can we change the time that has already passed. Time is universal. We cannot split it. And if we can't split it, we can't have multiple times.

In short, it's just time. A minute spent on one activity lasts exactly as long as a minute spent on another, no matter how different the two activities may be. Whether we spend an hour crawling along at a snail's pace in an endless traffic jam or zipping along the open highway, exactly 60 minutes will have passed. It is when we relate to time, experience it from the perspective of the present or relate to it reflectively, that we subjectively and qualitatively feel as if it is passing more quickly or more slowly. "Time flies when you're having fun" is not only a well-known expression but something that most of us have experienced. Our subjective experience may suggest otherwise, but time always moves at the same pace.

Semantically speaking, however, we have done something potentially very dangerous. Through our language, we have created the illusion that time *can* be divided. Specifically, the human mind has fallen foul of three semantic manipulations that place us at perpetual risk of losing our way in life if we don't deconstruct them.

The first manipulation is the notion that we can split time. We are exposed to this idea day in, day out through the media, at work, through our own language and that of others. It is reinforced every time we talk about 'work time', 'leisure time', 'quality time' and so on, terms that lead us to think that different kinds of time exist, each measured in its own way. Work takes place in one time, leisure in another. Yes, it is practical to think of time as divisible into categories and to label and describe them differently, but this manipulation of language has major existential consequences. The repetition of this language reinforces the idea that time can be split, and we begin to believe that the same is true of life.

This brings us to the second semantic manipulation. We only have one indivisible life. Just as there is only one universal and transitory time, there is also only one universal and transitory life. Of course, we spend that time and those lives on different things – on what we call work or family, for example. However, language shapes reality. As previously mentioned, the Thomas theorem states that, "If men define situations as real, they are real in their consequences." If we believe that time can be split, then we begin to manipulate ourselves and each other into believing that life can also be split. We start talking about working life and love life, our life as a parent, a life of leisure. But we live just one life, in one time.

Why is it so important to acknowledge this?

Well, if you think that you can split time, you believe that you can split life, and if you believe that, then you think you can split human beings. This brings us to the third and most dangerous semantic manipulation. We are relentlessly exposed to a rhetoric that describes us as a series of different people: a worker, a parent, a sibling, a lover. But the truth about each and every one of us is that when we look in the mirror, all of us – rare deformities or cognitive conditions notwithstanding – see just one person. We don't see an army of people staring back at us – a worker, a spouse, a sibling – just one body, containing one mind.

Of course, we have different roles associated with different responsibilities, but we are never different people. We are one person both when at work and at leisure. The worker, the parent and the sibling are the same person. Even in the extreme example discussed earlier, the British investment bankers didn't change from one person into another. They just coated their humanity with a layer of Teflon, thick enough to help them manoeuvre their consciences around the consequences of their actions. It may have been a practical reaction, but it was also a dangerous one. They were operating in a sector notorious for its high suicide rates.[17] Even the sturdiest frying pan eventually loses its nonstick coating.

A study by *Harvard Business Review* shows that the two things we regret most about our careers are taking a job just for the money and not leaving when we knew the time was right.[18] Bearing in mind these two findings, simply establishing existential distance from our work – whether through Teflon or sheer denial – doesn't seem to be a sustainable solution. Work is an existential and intimate part of our lives. It encroaches on our lives and makes an alarming number of us ill, not just by making excessive physical demands on us, which has long been the case, but by seducing us into believing that life can be split. Quite simply, we have conned ourselves into thinking that work isn't existential, but merely a practical requirement given form by a profession. Unfortunately, however – or perhaps fortunately – our minds and bodies are so primitively wired that they don't understand this division. As mentioned, language has facilitated the idea that we are different people: one at work, another at home. This makes it far easier to accept that work is not the source of meaning and happiness that it should be, considering how much of our time and sense of self we devote to it.

If we divide time, we divide life. And if we divide life, we divide ourselves. This split has caused and justified different demands being placed on different parts of life. We are led to believe that the needs and aspirations we have outside of work don't need to be accommodated and fulfilled when we are at work, and vice versa. We start talking about professional development on the one hand and personal development on the other, as if they were wildly different parts of our body and life. But we are just one person: a human being who should, of course, develop throughout life. When drawing up life's balance sheet, we don't enter items in separate personal and professional columns. Even if we did, there would still only be one total on the bottom line. All things being equal, when we ultimately take stock of our lives, we have a much greater chance of it being meaningful if we look at life as a coherent whole and focus on equilibrium in the totality of our lives rather than seeking to sub-optimize individual parts and dimensions of it.

Acknowledging that we are one person, living one life, in one time, presents current and potential workers with two fundamental questions. First, is the best and most meaningful way to spend our one life with somebody or something that we love? If the answer is yes, then why on Earth do we accept spending so much time on what we call work, where we are rarely surrounded by people or things that we love? At this point, I should interject that this call to arms is not directed at those trapped in an economic and social prison from which they cannot escape – those for whom life is a real struggle for survival. I can and will never demand anything of them. However, I do demand that the rest of us demonstrate solidarity and charity and help those people. My call to arms is directed at those who have the luxury of having 'resources'.

It is deeply paradoxical that we spend so much time on something that we do not love. It is making us ill and slowly but surely eroding our economy. No matter how thick the Teflon coating or how profound the semantic manipulation of the human mind, we cannot function as half-people. A person cannot be divided in two, either literally or existentially. We don't get up and go to work; we get up and go out into our lives. Work is just one spoke of the wheel, one facet among many. However, it takes up so much of our time that we must begin to insist that work be imbued with the same involvement, love and intimacy that we demand and crave in every other aspect of our lives. Work is an intimate and existential part of life. No matter how much we try to convince our minds to believe otherwise, work has a significant impact upon us. Because it is not *just* work – it is life.

SPEED IS THE NEW GOD

The ultimate goal for human beings must be to ensure that our lives are meaningful, not just satisfying or happy. There is no universal answer to the question of the meaning of life. It's no longer written in big neon letters that it is to be reunited with the Lord in the afterlife. We have been set free to find our own answers to life's most important questions. The problem, however, is that we are rarely asked to do so. As small children, we live carefree lives in which other people make decisions for us. At primary school, we focus on reading, writing and arithmetic. Later, at secondary school, the emphasis is on getting our foot on the next rung of the educational ladder or gaining the qualifications we need to find work. Increasingly, education resembles a conveyor belt. The sooner it churns us out into the world of work, the better. Many governments have introduced a range of measures aimed at speeding young people through education and into work. These include incentives that give youngsters an extra competitive advantage if they move on to higher education within a certain period of time of finishing school.

In short, haste has been elevated to the status of a god. We all need to get a move on. Nobody knows why, but it's crucial that we rush headlong through the system. We have to complete our education in the prescribed time, with as high a grade average as possible, so that we can be immediately spat out into a labour market that hails us as new 'talent', scatters rose petals at our feet, and trumpets a fanfare to celebrate our arrival at the life-long, carefree party that is work. The labour market offers salvation and endless blue skies and reveals the ultimate truth about the meaning of life. So, let's get cracking!

Most of us know that in reality, work is rarely that rosy. We forget to tell other people this, because we're too busy trying to live up to all sorts of external demands about how quickly and productively we should be living our lives. Another important truth that we as a society have conveniently been too busy to pass on is that there is no empirical evidence of a correlation between finishing your studies more quickly – or with outstanding grades – and living a happy and meaningful life. On the contrary, studies indicate that the number of young people who report to have wellbeing in life has fallen in recent years.[19] Surely, it's time to ask whether haste really is the right god to worship?

We are so close to time that, like St Augustine, we find it difficult to grasp the concept properly. As a result, it often runs away from us, even though we know that once it's gone, it's gone.

Things really start to go wrong when we begin to conflate time and money. The Industrial Revolution transformed the nature of work. Unlike humans, machines didn't need downtime. In principle, they could operate nonstop, as long as they had fuel and people to tend them. The longer the machines worked, the more they produced. Suddenly, every second counted. Time became a crucial parameter. Unlike more organic ways of working, it was now possible to assign very accurate values to time, in the form of lost production. Time became money, both of which can be saved, used or wasted. However, unlike time, which never returns, in principle there is no limit on how much money we can accumulate. Time is finite, but money is infinite. We should reflect this in the way we use the concepts, instead of bandying them about as if they were interchangeable, as we often do. Obviously, time is worth far more than money.

However, according to Professor Elizabeth Dunn of the University of British Columbia, we consistently behave as if the opposite were the case. Her work shows that if we give a representative sample of the population the option of a 20% pay raise, but one that comes with a catch – either a 25% longer working week or a 50% longer commute to work – one in two would take the job.[20] Little wonder, then, that we are in a hurry to conform to the image of the ideal worker, to make ourselves as attractive as possible in the labour market and to accumulate as much money as possible. To make matters worse, we confer high social status on those who have a lot of money. Conversely, having lots of time and no money is viewed as almost shameful. Despite the fact that the respondents in Dunn's study who valued money more than time reported significantly lower levels of satisfaction with their lives, we still value money more than time. The example also shows how greater global prosperity can exist side-by-side with increasing stress and anxiety. Greater prosperity was meant to solve our problems and therefore lessen our stress – that's why we worked so hard to achieve it, right? As Dunn points out, the greater the economic value you place on your time, the more you feel under time pressure.[21] The more money you earn, the more you feel that you don't have enough time.

Philosophically, it makes very little sense to rush to earn huge amounts of money in an attempt to enhance your quality of life, only to end up with no time and a lower quality of life. But that's exactly what we do. We value money more than time and in our pursuit of Mammon, we have elevated haste to the status of a god. Nonetheless, is there anything to be gained from studying how best to use our money?

Dunn shows that money *can* be used to buy a more satisfying life, as long as we use it to buy time. Her studies in Denmark, the Netherlands, Canada and the US reveal that spending money on time-saving services such as cleaning or gardening translates into a far higher sense of satisfaction than spending money on material goods. The first step is, therefore, to recognize that time *is* worth more than money.

We can also increase our awareness of how we use money by making it more visible. At its most basic, money is functional. We only really relate to it when it runs out. Only once there's no money left in our account are we reminded of its significance and what it means. The same applies to time. We only tend to reflect on how we use it when life reminds us that it doesn't last forever. When it comes to a lack of money, the worst-case scenario is that we end up bankrupt and insolvent, or perhaps worse still, having that fate exposed on reality TV. When it comes to time, however, the worst-case scenario is that we end up regretting the life that we have lived as a result of using it poorly, i.e., not spending it on things that endow our lives with meaning.

When we are 'broke', it is prudent to draw up a budget to see where we are bleeding money. What if we drew up a budget not for how we spend our money, but how we spend our time? Given how we rush headlong through life, would it be that outlandish to stop every now and then and take stock of how we spend our limited time? If time is worth more than money, it would make sense to budget both just as meticulously. Or even to budget time more meticulously than money.

The present flies by so quickly that it's difficult to prioritize what we do. However, the deathbed confessions described in the foreword should give us serious pause for thought about how we bring up our children and prepare them for life.

Given that we live the majority of our lives as adults, parenting and education are primarily about inculcating in our children a level of self-worth and sense of self that helps them cope with everything life throws at them while remaining true to themselves and finding meaning in life. Our responsibility as parents, teachers and politicians is to prepare children for life and not just to pass exams or find jobs. That's not what life is about. Life is about finding meaning, and you won't necessarily be able to do that just because you've learned square roots. I'm not saying that learning the three Rs and how to pass exams detracts from a young person's quality of life. However, those skills are – and always will be – secondary to the ability to navigate meaningfully through adult life. Ideally, our children will enter adulthood equipped with a wide variety of skills, such as speaking multiple languages fluently, solving complex mathematical equations and being able to talk about significant periods in human history – while also possessing integrity, having a zest for life and finding meaning in their existence. But it is pointless to have the secondary skills if you don't have the primary ones. While the former are useful, the latter are absolutely essential.

Naturally, we reward those who know their square roots. Indeed, we reward everyone who possesses skills that are in demand; in other words, skills that are of mutual benefit to both the individual and the system. What we fail to do is remind these skilled people that they should probably spend more time with their loved ones. We rarely tell them that they should be less concerned with meeting the expectations of others and that they should focus instead on living life on their own terms. But what would be the consequences of this? In the absence of an omnipotent god or an oracle to tell us the answer, we accept the role society has allocated to us. In the absence of any acknowledgment of who we are or who we want to be, we begin to covet what we think everyone else covets.

Psychologists call this phenomenon 'pluralistic ignorance'. If nobody really cares about a given norm, but everyone believes that everyone else cares about and accepts the norm, then nobody will dare breach it. In short, everyone believes because they think everyone else believes. We use this phenomenon to justify not doing what we think is right because everybody else is just carrying on as before. The problem is that 'everyone else' is only carrying on because that's what 'everyone else' is doing, which only reinforces the pluralistic ignorance. In principle, this can lead to a situation in which everyone disagrees with a given norm, but we all continue to comply with it because we think everyone else accepts it. We elevate haste to the status of a god and rush around like headless chickens because that's what those around us are doing.

The fact that we reward those who run fastest incentivizes us to run at least as fast because we crave the reward as well. The French psychoanalyst Jacques Lacan explored this phenomenon in greater depth.[22] We crave what we feel we lack; first and foremost, recognition and reward. If the system pats us on the back every time we hurry up, this encourages us to rush even more. However, according to Lacan, we crave more than just recognition. For him, our cravings are not our own but are instilled in us by what we think other people want. As such, they are often just a product of the virtues, morals and ideals that permeate our culture and upbringing. Given that haste is very much the god that defines those virtues, morals and ideals, it is hardly surprising that we are constantly in such a hurry. It's simply what our culture expects of us. The problem is that being in a hurry is not conducive to learning about ourselves. That takes space and reflection. It means being honest about yourself and your doubts; using your parents and teachers as a sounding board and asking questions more often than you give answers.

Nowadays, however, we don't educate people so that they *know who they are*. Rather, we educate them primarily so that they understand *what they can become*. We offer them insight into techniques and professions to make them as effective and attractive to employers as possible. In that sense, we've scarcely made any progress since 1872, when German philosopher Friedrich Nietzsche delivered the following critique of the purpose of the educational institutions of the day:

> The purpose of education, according to this scheme, would be to rear the most 'current' men possible, – 'current' being used here in the sense in which it is applied to the coins of the realm. The greater the number of such men, the happier a nation will be; and this precisely is the purpose of our modern educational institutions: to help everyone, as far as his nature will allow, to become 'current'; to develop him so that his particular degree of knowledge and science may yield him the greatest possible amount of happiness and pecuniary gain. [...] In this quarter all culture is loathed which isolates, which sets goals beyond gold and gain, and which requires time: it is customary to dispose of such eccentric tendencies in education as systems of

'Higher Egotism,' or of 'Immoral Culture – Epicureanism.' Indeed, the dominant morality of the day demands precisely the opposite; namely, a quick education so that one may swiftly become a money-earning being, but also a thorough education, so that one may become a very well-earning being.[23]

We need to consider whether our primary and secondary schools and universities should aim to produce adults capable of achieving happiness and meaning, or whether they are just there to feed the labour market. Today, we mainly educate people to be 'current', or marketable. We want people to be able to sell themselves on the market at as high a price as possible, in order to generate as much profit as possible for themselves and society, in the hope of achieving happiness and salvation. But we can't consume our way to a good life, because meaningfulness stems from something completely different. There is not enough wealth in the world to compensate for a meaningless life.

If we achieve high grades and qualifications and yet our humanity and self-knowledge are underdeveloped, we will be at a disadvantage not only in terms of living a good life but also in our endeavours to achieve above-average professional experiences. We should be more interested in the education system developing people of character than people with good grades who are ready to venture forth into the world of work. Regardless of how marketable we may be, or how diligently we have learned to generate the greatest profit from our personal level of knowledge, it is ultimately those who know themselves best who will find the shortest path to a meaningful life.

We have lost sight of the importance of pausing for thought, to reflect on whether our lives are on a meaningful path.

It is in such pauses that we, alone or with others, become a little wiser – not only about who we are, but just as importantly, about who we are not and will never be. We shouldn't fear the isolation to which Nietzsche refers. Indeed, it is a healthy respite from a life that is racing away from us, burning up time that will never come again. Solitude provides breathing space, a moment to look inside ourselves and figure out whether we are becoming who we want to be. In many ways, life is similar to music; without pauses, it would just be noise. It is the pauses between notes, the spaces between beats, that create the melody, the rhythm and the subtlety. The most valuable thing an education has to offer is not qualifications, but the opportunity to learn who you are. But developing this takes time – time that you must set aside in the one life that you live as the one person you are. The meaning of life can't just be to earn money, nor to race around worshipping the god of haste.

However, since our cravings, the recognition and the reward are all tied up with being as prepared as possible for work and to earn money, rather than being prepared for life as a self-aware being, it's difficult to break free from pluralistic ignorance, from what we believe others expect of us. A 2016 study of American college students[24] showed how the average final-year student spent four fewer hours per week socializing with friends and three fewer hours partying compared with 1987. That's seven fewer hours of social time every week – an hour a day in which they could be developing social skills, navigating personal relationships and learning to manage their own emotions.

Rushing around brings status, but leaves no spare time in which to be still. Perhaps Danish philosopher Søren Kierkegaard was on to something when he expressed his amusement at the meaninglessness of being busy:

> Of all ridiculous things, the most ridiculous seems to me, to be busy – to be a man who is brisk about his food and his work. Therefore, whenever I see a fly settling, in the decisive moment, on the nose of such a person of affairs; or if he is spattered with mud from a carriage which drives past him in still greater haste; or the drawbridge opens up before him; or a tile falls down and knocks him dead, then I laugh heartily. And who could help laughing? What, I wonder, do these busy folks get done? Are they not to be classed with the woman who in her confusion about the house being on fire carried out the firetongs? What things of greater account, do you suppose, will they rescue from life's great conflagration?[25]

We must not confuse being busy with being important or, even worse, with being meaningful. Being busy is often little more than a way to avoid dwelling on whether the things with which we are busy really *are* important. It is only once life throws us off course and offers us a diversion from our everyday chores that we seriously begin to account for how we spend our time. All too often, this requires a drawbridge to retract before us or a tile to fall on our head, metaphorically speaking. It is often only on our deathbed, liberated from the expectations and judgment of others, that we achieve a certain clarity of vision and perhaps experience regret. The sooner we arrive at such a moment of truth, the sooner we can recalibrate how we spend our time and ensure that we are working toward the right goals. However, that requires abandoning the prevailing virtues, morals and ideals of our culture. It requires that we do away with the career ladder in order to climb a completely different one every day – a ladder that does not lead to personal enrichment through recognition, certificates, titles or material wealth. Rather, it is a ladder of *self-respect*, the primary purpose of which is to create self-insight, which will create self-awareness, which leads to self-worth and then to self-respect.

2

THE LADDER OF
SELF-RESPECT

Are you a better-than-average driver? Probably not. Some of us have to be mediocre, some below average, some above average. Nonetheless, most of us don't let simple mathematics get in the way of our conviction that we are above average. Psychologists call it 'the better-than-average effect'. Statistical impossibility notwithstanding, we tend to think that we are above average. We are so confident in our own abilities that we are reluctant to hand control of our vehicles over to technology, even though evidence suggests that machines navigate better than people. This delusion extends far beyond our driving ability. Seven out of ten of us believe that we are a better friend than those around us. Six out of ten think that we are a better-than-average colleague. Just as many think that we are better partners than most other people.[26]

Clearly, our self-awareness is in need of recalibration. But then again, we rarely measure the quality of what we do against an objective standard. Opinions about what makes a good driver differ wildly. Is it someone who drives safely? Someone who drives efficiently? Someone who observes the rules of the road? Are polite Sunday drivers really better at it than boy racers? It's difficult enough to determine whether someone actually is a better-than-average driver, but defining a good friend, colleague or partner is much more complicated. There are many ways to do it and, in moments of hesitant uncertainty, we are quick to give ourselves and our abilities the benefit of the doubt. If nobody else is prepared to provide us with the recognition that we crave, we will give ourselves a slap on the back.

A group of researchers from the University of Southampton, Royal Holloway, the University of London and Ohio University spent some considerable time trying to identify the most objective, extreme example of this phenomenon.[27] They posed themselves the following question: which group of people is most closely associated with personality traits that are indisputably negative compared with the average? They came to the conclusion that, all things being equal, prison inmates would have difficulty competing with the rest of the population in terms of integrity, as they face the unmistakable consequences of their lack of scruples on a daily basis. They then interviewed 85 prisoners in English jails and asked them to evaluate themselves against a range of parameters.

They were asked to give themselves scores indicating the extent to which they were moral, trustworthy, honest, dependable, compassionate, generous, law-abiding, self-controlled and kind to others. First, they were asked to compare themselves with the average fellow prisoner, then with the average member of the public. Hardly surprisingly, they rated themselves as better than the average fellow inmate across all nine of the parameters – a clear example of 'the better-than-average effect'. More surprisingly, the prisoners *also* rated themselves as better than the average member of the public across eight of the nine parameters. They rated themselves as more moral, more trustworthy, more honest, more dependable, more compassionate, more generous, more self-controlled and more kind to others. Only in one category did they concede that they perhaps might not outperform the general public: being law-abiding. Even then, they didn't rate themselves as *less* law-abiding than the average member of the public but placed themselves on the *same* level as people not behind bars. People suspended from reality and deprived of their liberty as a consequence of their own actions nonetheless believe themselves to be more moral, trustworthy, honest, dependable, compassionate, generous, self-controlled and kind to others than people who are not behind bars.

The prisoners also consistently underestimated the probability of their reoffending upon release, further betraying a severe lack of self-awareness. Why do so many of us – not just criminals – think that we are better-than-average drivers, partners and law-abiding citizens, even though, statistically speaking, we have no reason to believe this? Where does this exaggerated confidence in our own abilities come from?

SELF-INSIGHT CREATES SELF-AWARENESS

In ancient Greece, people consulted the sacred Oracle of the Temple of Apollo at Delphi for advice and guidance on important decisions, as Apollo was the god of reason. Before they were allowed to lay themselves and their travails bare before the Oracle, they were confronted by the inscription 'Know thyself' on the marble walls of the temple, commanding them to confront their own selves, including their strengths and weaknesses. Only once they were armed with self-insight, including into their limitations, humanity and mortality, could they then turn to the Oracle and the gods for advice. It was considered a virtue to look inward, to first establish who you were and who you were not, before asking others to relate to you.

How many of us today can actually claim that we know who we are? How many of us can precisely, logically and coherently answer the question, "Who are you?" Most of us would reply, as if in a trance, by saying what what our job is – but running the fruit and vegetable department in a supermarket says more about 'what' you are than about 'who' you are. Who we are is a deep and profound question about our strengths, weaknesses and personality. When we ask another person *who* they are, and they respond by telling us *what* they are, we should – politely but firmly – remind them of the difference between the two and pose the question again. In reality, however, most of us don't know who we are, and so we accept a *what* answer to a *who* question. We are keen to avoid the question being turned back on us, which would expose the fact that we don't have a clue who we are either. We end up spending more time telling the other person about special offers on apples and opportunities for promotion than we do talking about *who* we are and listening to others' accounts of *who* they are.

The Danish author Karen Blixen, for many known under the pseudonym Isak Dinesen, said in 1957, "Within our whole universe the story only has the authority to answer that cry of heart of its characters, that one cry of heart of each of them: 'Who am I?'"[28]

To understand yourself or explain to others who you are, you must understand your own story. The important thing here is not our ability to distinguish between 'what' and 'who'. Of course, there is a certain value in using language more or less correctly, so that we are not forever explaining what we mean. However, the crucial point is that language is interlinked with culture. It is our culture that has shaped us and led to the trivial habit of thinking that if we don't know the answer to a question, we should just answer a different or similar one to avoid exposing our ignorance. We even reward people who are good at pretending to know things they don't. Think about oral exams or job interviews – we train ourselves and each other to steer any conversation toward topics with which we are more comfortable – even if they have very little to do with the matter at hand. If, every now and then, we slip up and betray our lack of understanding, it is acceptable to spin the story in a way that shows there was a happy ending anyway. We believe that openly acknowledging what we don't know and can't do will lead others to consider us weak. As a result, we have become anxious about exposing our limitations. They are simply not marketable.

What are the consequences of this as we leave the education system, pass through the eye of the needle at the job interview, and begin receiving feedback and participating in performance reviews? Do we suddenly find ourselves criticized for our flaws and weaknesses, in as detailed and profound a manner as we are praised for our strengths and achievements? Hardly. Unfortunately, management psychology and pedagogy have taught us that every piece of negative criticism must be offset by three pieces of positive feedback. In other words, we learn to spend three times as long recognizing and developing our strengths as we do recognizing and addressing our weaknesses. This is a misguided approach. What if the reality was the other way around and we had three things we had been no good at and only one thing that we had actually mastered? To compensate, do we then make up two nonexistent skills and ignore two failings?

Naturally, any criticism – whether given by a manager to an employee, a mother to a son or between friends – must be delivered sensitively, with a view toward helping the person being criticized to realize their full potential. However, our insistence on inventing or exaggerating positives in order to compensate for or play down negatives is unhealthy. It means we have an unrealistic starting point from which to learn to understand ourselves. At best, we gain access to the part of ourselves that is good at something, and which is rewarded and reinforced in the course of our lives, but we ignore the other parts of ourselves.

If we visit the Temple of Apollo with an overly positive self-perception, this will limit the guidance and advice available to us. In other words, if we arrive full of self-confidence – possessing absolute faith in our own abilities – we leave again with insight that only reinforces that self-confidence. So, we stop visiting the Oracle to find answers and instead go there for affirmation. We don't think we need to read the inscription on the temple wall.

This is a bad habit. It means that our self-insight never translates into self-awareness. Instead, it lingers on as self-conceit. Excessive self-confidence, constantly fuelled and inflated by positive self-insight, means that, despite all exhortations to engage in more balanced introspection about our place in the world, we don't permit ourselves any negative self-insights, even in a prison cell. If even prison offers no reflective space in which to recognize ourselves and our weaknesses, it is unsurprising that there is no such space in our car, in our friendships, in our workplaces or in our marriages.

When self-insight is only bound up with self-confidence, it descends into self-sufficiency, and we ultimately become self-glorifying oracles, constantly overestimating ourselves, driven by an intoxicating rush of confidence in ourselves and our own thoughts and ideas. Occasionally, we get things wrong, but we are told just to forget it and move on. We are also told that, statistically speaking, our lives should be full of happiness, which means that there is even less incentive to spend much time dwelling on aspects of ourselves that are less than optimal. We really don't want to be seen as unhappy when the norm demands the opposite. As a result, slowly but surely, we become anxious about appearing imperfect and unhappy.

Only perfect people can live perfect lives, though, and the perfect person has never existed. All of us are born with limitations, whether physical, intellectual or social. By definition, imperfect people can only live imperfect lives. This is precisely what the inscription on the marble wall of the Temple of Apollo sought to remind those seeking counsel – that they were anything but divine. Similarly, being confined to prison should remind us that we are anything but law-abiding.

Overestimating ourselves and indulging in self-glorification are not the only things that prevent self-insight from becoming self-awareness. Self-glorification has an evil twin called self-contempt. If we approach the world with a lack of faith in our abilities, if our self-insight consists exclusively of negativity, and if we focus on everything we can't do, then self-contempt takes over. This leads us to develop a predominantly negative self-understanding. We forget to take into account all the things that we can do and end up with another form of false self-awareness – this time, one that is extremely depressing and negative.

Self-contempt is particularly noticeable when we manipulate ourselves and others into believing that life can be split. When we split time, life and ourselves, we forget to look at the big picture. When we divide up our lives, we start to tell ourselves that the man sitting next to us would be a more attentive father, that the woman who lives down the road would be a sexier wife and that the manager in that other department is more competent. Instead of evaluating our lives and ourselves in a holistic and coherent manner, we split ourselves up and inevitably end up being wholly imperfect. But nobody can be the world champion in everything. Usain Bolt may be the world's fastest 100-metre sprinter, but he wasn't talented enough to fulfil his ambition of playing for Real Madrid.

In other words, you can't be in the top quartile for everything. If you compare yourself against perfection in all aspects of life, it becomes easy to slip into a downward spiral of contempt for yourself and your shortcomings.

Conversely, if our self-insight takes into account only our positive qualities and skills, we are at risk of believing that life can be perfect – and even, perhaps, that we are well on the way to achieving this perfection. But we can't be beautiful all the time. We can't always know best. We can't be the parent who feeds their children the most nutritious food possible every single day. We can't be society's most dedicated and conscientious citizen 365 days a year. And we most certainly cannot be all things to all people all of the time. However, when we constantly remind ourselves and each other how good and clever we are, we inflate each other's self-confidence. We actually begin to believe not only in impossibilities such as splitting life, but even that we are in the upper quartile. Vice versa, if we continuously doubt our abilities and fill ourselves with self-contempt, we actually begin to believe that everyone else ranks above us in the upper quartile for everything.

Every step we take on the path toward healthy self-awareness must be trodden honestly. Surrounding yourself with people who relate to you as you truly are is a prerequisite for developing healthy self-insight. If our self-insight is dishonest, it creates an unstable foundation upon which only distorted self-awareness can be built. When we collectively acknowledge and affirm insights that either don't exist at all or have been greatly exaggerated, we are attempting to nourish ourselves, psychologically and existentially, with either self-glorification or self-contempt.

The 'Dunning-Kruger effect',[29] a widely recognized phenomenon in social psychology, means that people who lack skills or knowledge in a given field consistently and significantly overestimate their capabilities. They simply don't know enough to recognize how much they don't know. We often convince ourselves that our knowledge is extensive, or our attitude is correct, even when there is little or no evidence to support this. We are also prone to confirmation bias where we invariably regard facts that support our understanding or choices as more credible than those that challenge them.

For a healthy self-awareness, our self-insight must encompass both confidence *and* doubt. We must seek knowledge not only of our positive qualities but also of the less desirable characteristics that we inevitably possess. Only once we have mustered up the courage to confront our dark and shameful traits as readily as we remind ourselves of the bright and shiny ones, will we succeed in fully realising ourselves as whole human beings. If we cultivate only one type of insight, we will find ourselves on a slippery slope that exponentially accelerates a self-perpetuating belief in either our genius or our uselessness. In either case, the destination is the same – loneliness. Self-confidence can easily become self-centredness, while self-contempt can easily become self-destruction. Both ultimately lead to isolation.

For each step that we take in either of these directions, the path back to true self-awareness becomes longer and more difficult, and we will never reach the next rung on the ladder of self-respect – self-worth.

It is absolutely necessary that we surround ourselves with people who can honestly contribute to our self-awareness and help us strike a healthy balance between confidence and doubt.

SELF-AWARENESS CREATES SELF-WORTH

On 28 March 2007, 29-year-old goalkeeper Robert Enke finally made his debut for the German national football team in a friendly match against Denmark. It had been obvious since he was a child that Enke had a flair for goalkeeping. Nor was he a stranger to elite sport, as his father was a successful hurdler and his mother played handball. He was a regular in the national youth teams from the age of 15 and made his debut in the German national league, the Bundesliga, at 20. He played for big clubs abroad like Benfica and Barcelona – with mixed success – before returning to Germany, where he was goalie and later captain of Hannover 96. During the 2004–2005 and 2008–2009 seasons, he was voted the best keeper in the league by his peers in the other clubs. He was, without doubt, one of the most talented goalkeepers of his generation and attracted interest from some of the biggest clubs in the world, including Arsenal, Manchester United and Atlético Madrid.

In the run-up to the 2010 World Cup, Enke finally looked like he had a chance of being the number one for the national team, which was the ultimate breakthrough on the biggest stage of all. However, it wasn't to be.

On 8 November 2009, Robert Enke, then 32 years old, played in a home game in front of 50,000 people. His team sneaked a draw with a goal in the final minutes and left the pitch to cheers from the home crowd. Two days later, on 10 November 2009, Enke trained as usual in the morning but then didn't show up in the afternoon. That evening, his teammates, the fans and the world media were shocked to hear that Enke had committed suicide by throwing himself in front of a regional express train.

What very few people knew about Robert Enke was that he suffered from anxiety, and had been diagnosed with clinical depression twice, in 2003 and 2009. In 2003, he was dropped by Barcelona and developed a morbid fear of failure. He kept it very quiet, sought treatment and slowly but surely fought his way out of it – at least at first. Three years later, his life took the most tragic turn imaginable when his two-year-old daughter died of a congenital heart defect. But even then, he managed to keep the depression at bay. It only returned when he suffered a hand injury. Then, in November 2009, for reasons that remain unclear, he suffered a relapse and chose to take his own life.

The point is not why Robert Enke took his own life. It is that even one of the most talented players of his generation, a man of such indisputable and feted skill, could have had such incredibly low self-worth that he thought life was no longer worth living. Statistically, he still had two-thirds of his life ahead of him, which he would in all probability have spent in the upper income quartile.

Self-confidence and self-doubt are linked to our actions and behaviour to the extent to which we feel that we have mastered what we spend our time doing, whether we have faith in what we do and our ability to achieve the results we want. Self-confidence and self-doubt are very much conditioned by our surroundings – our parents, teachers, colleagues and managers. Self-confidence is a hollow concept, as our level of self-confidence is often determined by the last thing we did. It doesn't matter how much of it we accumulate in the course of our lives, because as soon as our abilities and characteristics are challenged, we lose it again.

Given that the perfect person is yet to tread this planet, none of us will ever get through life without encountering resistance. This is particularly true in the world of sport, especially for goalkeepers. One mistake at a crucial moment is the difference between success and failure or being the hero or the villain. Entire careers are defined in a single instant. This is where self-worth becomes essential. While self-confidence is linked to our actions and results, self-worth is rooted in our identity. It is the experience of having a basic value as a human being that generates self-worth. Once self-insight has generated self-awareness, it is our self-worth that constantly reminds us of our value, irrespective of our current level of self-confidence. In the moments of failure that we all experience – relationship breakdowns, redundancies and so on – it is self-worth that regulates the impact upon our overall sense of our own intrinsic value. Without self-worth, we leave this vital role in life to our self-confidence, which is only concerned with the immediate past, with the last thing we did and, as such, is extremely fragile.

The reason for this is that self-confidence does not lead to self-worth, or at least not to such an extent that our obvious and acknowledged professional qualities make us feel sufficiently worthwhile. It is not self-confidence that makes people respect themselves and their lives so much that they find life too worthwhile to commit suicide or spend it on activities that hinder them in finding the meaning for which they are searching. It is not confidence in our skills, professional competencies or attributes that endows life with meaning. If that were the case, technically skilled individuals would have achieved higher levels of self-worth and found meaning in life. Suicide is often the most extreme and most visible consequence of low self-worth. It is a horrible enough thought that somewhere in the world, somebody commits suicide every 40 seconds (800,000 people p.a.).[30] But it's even more sobering that for each person who succeeds in taking their own life, nine others try and fail, and many more think about it. Not to mention the countless others who teeter on the verge every day. For them, too, this is not due to any lack of professional recognition or acknowledgement of their technical skills. Our education system and labour market make a point of constantly honouring us with symbols, grades and titles to maintain our self-confidence by confirming that we are indeed good at something.

As a consequence, a zero-mistake culture has taken root throughout the education system and we have tied our self-worth too closely to our achievements. Our worth – or lack thereof – is based solely on results. We also know that in the world of work, self-confidence, impeccability and high grades are rewarded more than self-worth, self-awareness and character. As such, we are more intensely focused on the former rather than the latter. The reason for this is simply that it generates larger and more 'marketable' returns.

What if we were to reward self-worth rather than self-confidence? This would lead to the emergence of a generation whose interest in knowing themselves would be as intense and focused as their current drive to learn algebra and grammar. The first rung on the ladder of self-respect is self-insight. But unless self-insight is rooted in honesty, we will never even climb that high. And because honesty takes time, it is in the economy's short-term interest to pump people full of self-confidence, so that they jump straight into the rat race and scurry around like everybody else around them. Much of the growth that we chase so eagerly will be used to pay for the treatment of the increasing number of people suffering from stress, anxiety, depression and loneliness, as well as associated lifestyle diseases, all caused by our eagerness to generate growth.

It all starts with the writing on the wall in the Temple of Apollo. Only with sufficient insight into ourselves do we recognize who we are and are not. When we know our strengths and weaknesses, we take power away from both self-confidence and self-contempt. Our value is not tied to our most recent failure or success, but to the sum total of our being.

We live one life, in one time, as one person. We should not let our house of cards topple because of a single misstep, nor should we build its foundation on something as fragile as self-confidence or self-doubt. Self-insight leads to self-awareness, which leads to self-worth.

But how can we use this knowledge about ourselves and the self-worth it generates to withstand the friction caused by daily encounters with a world that demands perfection? If we acknowledge that life must be considered – and lived – as a coherent whole, which can't be split, how do we ensure that there is consistency between our purpose and the life we actually live, across all of our roles and responsibilities? In other words, how do we ensure that, when we are on our deathbed, we will look back on our life and career with a sense of pride? Self-insight, self-awareness and self-worth are not enough. We need to use these attributes, day in and day out, in everything we do by practising self-respect.

SELF-WORTH CREATES SELF-RESPECT

Self-insight leads to self-awareness, which leads to self-worth, which leads to self-respect. That is the ladder we must climb every day if we want to find our way to a meaningful existence. It's not enough to know who you are and recognize that you have a value if you don't deploy that knowledge and recognition with respect amid the trials and tribulations of everyday life. Self-worth does not become self-respect until we act upon our knowledge of what we can and cannot do, and our acknowledgement of who we are and are not. That is not easy.

For example, how do we react when we receive an invitation to a dinner party that we don't think will be a meaningful way to spend our valuable time? Either we make up a pathetically poor excuse – we are double-booked, or our partner won't allow it – or we grudgingly accept for fear of the response our refusal would elicit. You might, of course, be in for a pleasant surprise – but how often have you started to feel pangs of regret halfway through the starter, as you run out of small talk and have to sit there, feeling awkward and impatient, watching the clock tick until the earliest possible moment when going home wouldn't be considered too impolite? The tension ratchets up until you are eventually released. You fly out of the door and dash home to throw yourself on the couch, revelling in the sensation of being liberated from the stifling straitjacket of politeness.

Similarly, in a work situation, how often do we allow ourselves to spend hour after hour in tedious, poorly planned and unproductive meetings? How often do we find ourselves surrounded by people or tasks that drain our energy and waste our time, and yet we say nothing? According to the *Harvard Business Review*, more than 70% find meetings unproductive and inefficient[31] – but how many of us have enough self-respect to leave or cancel a meeting that has no benefit to anyone or anything? Our world isn't very accommodating to people who bear themselves with self-respect. How do we react, for example, when someone opts out of something? Do we thank them for their courage, and their ability to know themselves, their needs and their limitations? Hardly. Usually, we either exert moderate peer pressure or adopt a cynical distance. If someone says that their time would be better spent on something else, it might reveal that we are uninteresting or that we should really consider spending our time on something else.

It hurts when we are challenged about whether our lives have as much existential meaning as they could potentially have. This is especially true of those for whom climbing the career ladder has cost them dearly. Often, the greater the success, the greater the fear of losing all those years of hard-won seniority. Success breeds the need for even more success. To maintain conformity, we either exclude or put down those who opt out. But seniority has no value for self-respect. All it quantifies is how long we have endured something, with no indication of whether that endurance has been meaningful. Ultimately, we are defined by the sum of our actions. It is via self-respect that we seek to minimize the distance between our knowledge of who we are and the reality of what we do every day.

We only live one life in one time as one person – one life that is transitory, in a time that is universal. The time we waste is the same, no matter what we waste it on. If we waste an hour on an inconsequential meeting, that means less sand in the hourglass, less time to realize the life that we want. If we know who we are and find dignity in that, we should always respect ourselves enough not to tolerate wasting any more of our one life than is necessary; and we should treat every other life we encounter with the same respect. If we are curious, rather than judgmental, about the person who has opted out based on their self-respect, we have a chance to find out who they really are. It is also a good short-cut to determine, as quickly and as honestly as possible, whether we share a purpose in life that makes it worth spending parts of it together.

On their deathbeds, people who have climbed the ladder of self-respect every day are less likely to regret the life they have lived than those who devoted their time to climbing self-confidence's greasy career pole.

THE EXISTENTIAL IMMUNE SYSTEM

In the opening scene of Paul Thomas Anderson's film *Magnolia*, 17-year-old Sydney Barringer tries to commit suicide by jumping off a nine-storey apartment block. In his pocket is a suicide note that he believes – once the law of gravity, according to his plan, has engineered an abrupt encounter between his body and the pavement – will unambiguously confirm the intention behind his action. What Barringer doesn't know is that a few days earlier, a safety net was strung out at first-floor level to protect a team of window cleaners who were working their way up the building.

The net would have halted his descent and saved Sydney's life if it weren't for the fact that he was shot in the stomach on the way down. Because while Barringer is standing on the edge of the roof, a dramatic scene unfolds in an apartment three floors below. The neighbours are used to the couple shouting and bawling at each other, and the husband and wife frequently threaten each other with hunting rifles and handguns. They've just never acted on the threats. However, on this particular day, as the wife threatens her husband, the weapon goes off by accident. The bullet misses her husband, goes through the window and hits Sydney Barringer, whose plummeting body passes the window just at that nanosecond. The shot is lethal. All the safety net does is save the city from a major cleaning job.

Later, once the police have successfully connected the two events, the couple are confronted with the horrible and complicated news. Both deny having loaded the firearm and claim to have had no intention of doing anything other than threaten each other. It subsequently transpires that the weapon had been loaded, not by them but by their teenage son. Exhausted by his parents' endless conflict, he saw no other solution than to load the weapon in the hope that one of them would kill the other.

What the woman who fired the gun doesn't know is that her son had decided to take his own life that very day by throwing himself from the roof of the building where they live. Faye Barringer is charged with the murder of her son, Sydney, who, bizarrely, directly contributed to his own death, albeit not quite as planned. His suicide attempt may have failed, but he succeeded in murdering himself.

Sydney Barringer's fate reflects two truths about the conditions that we all definitely share. While suicide and violent parents blight far too many people's lives, they are, fortunately for most people, not the common denominator.

The first truth is that we will all die. We sometimes talk about it, but not very often, and usually accompanied by an awkwardly cheery quip about not wanting to tempt fate. But sometimes, illness or accident forces us to acknowledge that life *is* finite and this usually gives us perspective, direction and priority. It reminds us that life comes to an end.

The second truth from which none of us is excluded, but which we rarely talk about or touch on, is that no matter how long, prosperous and educated a life we live and have in front of us, life will be unpredictable. It doesn't matter how much you educate yourself, structure, plan, prepare or turn up on time. We don't choose our parents, nor therefore the social, economic or geographical circumstances that form the backdrop and starting point for our existence. No one can avoid unpredictability, no matter how much we may coat ourselves with Teflon. The unpredictability of life undeniably means a certain possibility of stress. But we have a tendency to believe that we can make unpredictability disappear by simply educating ourselves even more or working even harder. But we can't train or work our way out of unpredictability. It is an unavoidable fact of life. It can be reduced, but never removed completely. So how do you hedge your bets in a transient and unpredictable life? The people best equipped to cope with life's coincidences are those who know and respect themselves. Even if you do not know what tomorrow will bring, you know yourself well enough that whatever life throws at you, you know what you want and don't want, what you can and can't do.

These days, there is huge focus on biological and economic immune systems. Health and wealth are considered the means by which to achieve a long and prosperous life. But, as previously mentioned, this attitude coexists with poorer existential health. How, then, do we build up an existential immune system to ensure that our lives are not only long and prosperous but acceptable to us and our fellow human beings?

This brings us back to the discussion of 'good'. When we acknowledge both that life has an end and that the path to it will be unpredictable, then happiness is something that emerges from our encounters with unpredictability. Whether our fate is positive or negative, fate itself must not be allowed to define whether we live a good life. After all, we cannot control its fluctuations. What we can control is how we tackle the unpredictability of life. And this is where meaning comes in; it acts as our existential immune system. When we are afflicted by pressure or grief, meaning is what makes us able to withstand and cope with the stress that undeniably arises from life's downs. When we are blessed with joy or happiness, meaning is what makes us able to cope with the euphoria that undeniably arises from life's ups and all the while retain our self-awareness because we know that it is not associated with the unpredictability *per se.*

Self-insight leads to self-awareness, which leads to self-worth, which leads to self-respect. This is the ladder that we must help ourselves and others climb every day. The goal of life is neither satisfaction nor happiness because, as guiding principles for our civilization, they haven't taken us where we need to go. We must, as often as possible, seek a deep sense of meaning in the one life we live.

3

INHUMAN
MANAGEMENT

What is the biggest threat to the modern human being's existential immune system? What stops us from experiencing the meaning in our lives that we need? No matter whether we use time or effect as the measuring stick, our jobs are the most obvious place to start looking for answers. Mathematically speaking, optimizing the part of our lives spent at work will produce the highest return, not only because work is our biggest investment in terms of time, but also because it has such a fundamental influence on the rest of our lives and is the source of much of our sense of meaninglessness. In far too many cases, work leads to – or greatly accelerates – stress, anxiety, depression and loneliness.

Much of the blame for this must be laid at the feet of managers who are incapable of making it clear to themselves or their staff what is meaningful about the job, or simply don't give a hoot, because meaning isn't one of the key performance indicators on which their salaries are based. A Danish study[32] suggests that more than half of people who opt to leave jobs cite lousy management as the main reason. The structures and frameworks that physically and mentally constrain us every single day are also cited as a major reason for staff leaving. One in three people mentions a poor psychological working environment. This is mentioned by more people than low wages or long working hours.

So, why are so many managers so bad at their jobs that they trigger stress, anxiety, depression and loneliness in their employees? And how did we end up in a situation where more people resign to escape a job than are lured away by a more attractive one? For too many people, their jobs are demotivating and lead to poor mental health. We need an in-depth examination of management infrastructure as a whole.

It is no surprise that work has such a huge impact on well-being. It is mainly at work that we are weighed and measured every day. Performance reviews, compensation and promotions are all frequent sources of either self-confidence (if we receive praise and acknowledgment) or self-doubt (if we do not). It doesn't even take censure or criticism to push us down the path of self-doubt. We are so pumped full of self-confidence that often just a momentary lack of recognition is enough to put a dent in our self-worth.

In the absence of feedback, we fill the silence with noisy questions, such as, "Am I not good enough? Am I about to be sacked?" Or at least we do if our existential immune system isn't strong enough to remind us that we have intrinsic value, irrespective of our most recent performance review or payslip. How often do we ask our closest family members to rate our performance over the last three months on a scale of one to five? How often do our parents call us in for a performance review to evaluate how we are developing in relation to the goals they have set for us? How often do we sit down with our closest friends and take stock of whether they deserve a promotion or even demotion? Do we usually hold formal exit interviews with our exes and arrange outplacement courses for them? Has anybody ever drawn up a personality profile or asked to see a GPA before choosing a spouse? Probably not. And yet measures like these are a routine, almost daily part of life at work. We measure and evaluate our performance at work with surgical precision and manic frequency, yet rarely do so in our day-to-day lives. Shouldn't we be even more systematic and serious about how we manoeuvre through life than about how we do so at work? After all, what's more important: recognition and success at work, or love and meaning in life? Everybody but the undiagnosed workaholic would probably (and sensibly) say the latter.

Acknowledging the complexity of life leads to two key questions. First, should it not be meaning and love that occupy our minds and form the basis for our self-evaluations? Second, should we not evaluate our jobs according to how much they help us find meaning and love in life? Do our jobs help us learn more about the purpose of our lives? Do they develop our level of self-insight and self-awareness? How good are we at creating meaningfulness for our colleagues? These types of questions are far more important indicators of the robustness of our existential immune system than any workplace assessment or performance review. Nor should these questions be the exclusive preserve of the so-called 'creative class'. Whether you are production staff, an office worker or a university graduate, I cannot see why you shouldn't have the same right to strive for a meaningful life.

However, regardless of how much time and space work occupies, and the fact that it is indisputably an existential and intimate part of our lives, we are led to believe the opposite. We have, quite simply, developed a language that dehumanizes and diminishes our hopes of intimacy, and bogs us down in the idea that work is incapable of being existential or intimate. We're told that we should think about work in purely professional and technical terms, as these are the parameters on which we are evaluated and paid.

Take one of management theory's most successful recent linguistic inventions: Human Resource Management. The concept originated from a period in mid-20th-century American management when people started slowly to be redefined as a resource – akin to raw materials, property, liquid assets and reputation – that companies must acquire in order to gain a competitive edge. Like so many other innovations from the US, the rest of the world was keen to adopt the concept as if it were the most natural thing in the world, so much so that every self-respecting organization, private or public, now has its own HR department.

This global import of Human Resource Management was done with the best of intentions, but please consider the literal meaning of the term – the administration of humans as resources. What does it imply if human resources are administered in the same way as other resources? Traditionally, a resource is something you extract, exploit and consume in order to obtain a competitive advantage. That's fine when we are discussing sources of energy, but it takes a somewhat skewed moral compass to believe that people are merely things to be exploited. To reduce human beings to resources is to dehumanize them. Luckily, we tend to use the abbreviation HR, perhaps in a subconscious attempt to ignore the tragic irony that seldom has a term sounded quite so inhuman. No matter how human the work of any given HR department actually is, the reckless abandon with which the phrase is bandied around is problematic. No wonder we coat our identities in Teflon when we are told time and again to devote our bodies, time and intellect to our work, then go home exhausted, fall asleep and get up again the next morning, barely revitalized and ready to be exploited once more to make sure the organization is competitive.

What happens when we use terminology and strategies to refer to human beings that originally referred to assets? In the worst-case scenario, the consequences can be fatal. In 2008–2009, 35 employees of France Telecom (now Orange) chose to take their own lives.[33] Union reps placed the blame squarely at the door of the company's extensive reorganization programme, also supported by suicide notes left by employees. For many at the company, sweeping compulsory changes to jobs or workplaces were too much to swallow. A researcher from the University of Leeds studied 82 suicide notes written by employees of three companies between 2005 and 2015. Most of them cited work as the main reason for their decision. Restructuring and redeployment were recurring themes.[34]

If we take an inanimate asset or resource and move it from one place to another, it has limited or no effect on how long it will remain useful and productive. We can move machines around with impunity. But not people. When we move people, we are also moving their whole being, psyche and all. People are far more fragile than machines. They are sensitive to the disruption caused by new surroundings, new responsibilities, new colleagues, new targets, a new corporate culture and new managers. Human beings aren't technologies or machines to be exploited. No matter how much we coat ourselves and each other in Teflon, we cannot avoid the fact that beneath our armour plating are minds that think, sense and remember what they are made to endure.

WORK-LIFE (IM)BALANCE

A study conducted in the UK in 2015[35] asked tens of thousands of people to record when they felt the highest and lowest levels of wellbeing and happiness. The researchers compiled a list of the top 40 activities. At the top was making love, followed by things like the theatre, dancing and gigs. Quite simply, the best times of our lives are spent with the people or activities that we love. At the bottom of the list, just above being ill in bed, was work. Chores like cleaning, standing in a queue and paying bills were all considered far greater sources of wellbeing and happiness than paid work. It's no surprise that love and intimacy give us the greatest pleasure, but it's shocking that the only thing to rank lower than going to work was being ill.

This should alarm every politician who understands that the national economy depends on people going to work and being as productive as possible. The problem is that society is weighed down by a political elite incapable of doing more than intone the mantra about 'making work pay'. Your job may be bad for you, make you ill and kill you, but cheer up, at least you'll be paid while it lasts.

We know that people who find their work meaningful are willing to work for lower wages. Higher wages are, in effect, often a form of compensation for a lack of meaning, a concept originating from Latin that implies not only evening something out but also making up for something. Something has gone fundamentally wrong if we are paying people more to put up with the abyss of meaninglessness that work creates. We would be wise to look more closely at work itself. How did we come to the conclusion that it is innately a bad thing and that we should look to other aspects of life for satisfaction, happiness and meaning?

It is a view that revolves around the concept of *work-life balance*, which implies that life can be split – something that is absurd and a logical impossibility. If work, viewed in isolation, is seen as a source of stress, anxiety and depression, and therefore intrinsically unhealthy, it makes no sense to talk about a healthy balance between 'work' and 'life'.

Such a balance can, by definition, never be healthy! More importantly, manufacturing a split in our existence between 'work' and 'life' is meaningless from an existential perspective. A 'balance' is either an equilibrium between two alternatives or a spot in the middle of a continuum between two extremes, which doesn't help make the picture any more understandable. The opposite of 'life' is 'death', but it makes no sense to talk about a balance between the two. Only zombies and vampires in fiction enjoy the privilege of being the living dead. The rest of us have to make do with being either alive or dead.

The distinction is, of course, easier to understand if we think of the opposite of work in pragmatic rather than linguistic terms. After all, it is a tad harsh to think of work as analogous to death. Even so, we cannot avoid the fact that the concept of 'work-life balance' not only positions a third of our lives in opposition to the other two-thirds, but it does so in a way that leaves nobody in any doubt that the first third (work) is an unpleasant, even harmful necessity in an existence nourished in reality by its opposite. This leaves us with only two options: either take up permanent residence in our self-made purgatory (at least until we retire or die) or drop out of the labour market.

Instead of rushing to the conclusion that it is work *per se* that is the source of our misery, we should look instead at its specific form and content. For example, we know that we enjoy paid work twice as much if we're able to work from home.[36] This makes it relevant to look at how we work, how we give our workload meaning, and how we work and manage ourselves and others. Doing so reveals that work in itself is not the problem and that it is highly probable that work-related stress, depression, anxiety and loneliness are not inevitable consequences of work as a phenomenon but are due to its content and form and the pronounced lack of meaning in both.

If work is so devoid of humanity, love and intimacy then, of course, it will not be something that we want to associate with our lives. Real life takes place in 'private time', in 'private lives', as 'private people', as opposed to work, which takes place during 'working hours', in 'working lives', as 'working people'. Even though the Teflon-coating approach can be a practical way to protect our intellect and identity against total exploitation, it's not very conducive to achieving a sense of meaning in life if we can only pursue this in the hours between work and sleep. Quite simply, we have deluded ourselves and others that it's enough to experience intimacy and love between waking up and going to work, and then again between getting home from work and going to bed. But the human psyche just doesn't work like that. We can't take such long breaks from intimacy and still expect life to be meaningful. We can't suspend our need for love for half of our waking hours and think that's enough. And yet, somehow, work has become a break from life. It is something we need to balance with life because we don't want it to take up too much space – the more space it takes up, the less life there is left to live. This makes it practical to be able to divide life up into working time and leisure time, as long as we are talking about work as the opposite of life.

But life isn't about balancing roles and identities. The main thing is to find meaning in the one single, transient life available to us. It is about ensuring that we look back on our life with the fewest possible regrets. Work-life balance is one of the most dangerous concepts ever devised. It tries to trick us into believing that life can be divided, and so can we.

LEAVE ME IN PEACE

In a situation where a company takes every opportunity to exploit its human resources, the desire for peace, quiet and distance is in many ways a necessity. But it doesn't have to be like that. If your employer has a decent, humane management style – and luckily, many do – there's absolutely no reason to build defensive fortifications around your 'private life'. But the workplace is just not organized as a place to give and receive love. On the contrary, they are places where we give and receive Human Resource Management. And we definitely need less of that. We need a break from it. Once an organization views people in terms of their potential, instead of as resources to be exploited, then it also begins to share the moral responsibility for protecting and realising that potential. This joint responsibility, if administered with care, will also mitigate the need for peace and balance, as it will also create space for life at work.

The structures and strategies inflicted on us are one thing. Management is another. Any discussion of our work, and of what fuels our motivation, joy and meaning in day-to-day life, will usually turn to our line managers. This is no great surprise. They are the people who exert the greatest influence on whether our day-to-day work endows our lives with meaning. It also explains why bad management is one of the main reasons people seek new pastures or think about doing so. 'Employees don't leave workplaces, they leave managers' is more than just a platitude. It reflects the fact that the main management or leadership style we encounter plays a significant role in how we feel about our work. Before we can address that phenomenon, it is essential to understand the difference between management and leadership.

DEARTH OF MORALITY

In 1977, American researcher Abraham Zaleznik wrote a landmark article[37] about the difference between management and leadership. He argued that the two concepts are based on fundamentally different ideas about employees. In the article, which was published in *Harvard Business Review*, Zaleznik wrote, "Managers embrace process, seek stability and control, and instinctively try to resolve problems quickly – sometimes before they fully understand a problem's significance. Leaders, in contrast, tolerate chaos and lack of structure and are willing to delay closure in order to understand the issues more fully."

What is interesting is that, based on these definitions, the vast majority of organizations practise management rather than leadership. To be effective, an organization needs both, but the evidence suggests that leadership has yet to make its big breakthrough. At the moment, there is no movement calling for the workplace to nurture employees with the poetry and intimacy they need.

Perhaps the reason for this lack of demand is to be found back at the Temple of Apollo at Delphi. After all, how many management textbooks state on page one that managers should know themselves before dealing with anybody else? Precious few. In psychology, it is generally acknowledged that human beings tend to overestimate their own abilities vastly. It's reasonable to assume that this is true of managers too. But how many organizations reward managers for acknowledging their mistakes and weaknesses? Even fewer. And how many managers are evaluated on the basis of how well they know themselves? None.

Some companies and organizations do, in fact, hold managers responsible for their staff evaluating their management positively and impose sanctions if necessary. However, this is merely cosmetic and the employee's sense of meaning in their work is often decoupled from the demands made on the management.

Little wonder, then, that managers are only interested in management. They are expected to manage their staff in the same way as the company's other strategically important resources – in order to generate growth and profit as cost-effectively as possible. As well as failing to focus on leadership, managers are not trained to help other people or themselves climb the ladder of self-respect or to make work meaningful. They are expected to manage on the basis of well-defined targets that have nothing whatsoever to do with creating a fundamental sense of meaning for the people for whom they are responsible.

How did we end with a generation of managers so incompetent? In 1969 Canadian psychologist Laurence J. Peter published the book 'The Peter Principle'[38] containing the famous principle that "In a hierarchy every employee tends to rise to his level of incompetence." The book was originally intended as a satiric exposure of why so many managers are incompetent, but its basic idea has since been investigated more rigorously. In 2018, professors Alan Benson, Danielle Li and Kelly Shue published their research[39] testing the validity of The Peter Principle. They analysed sales professionals' performance and promotion practices inside 214 American organizations, concluding, perhaps unsurprisingly, that the best sales professionals were in fact more likely to be promoted. But, more surprisingly, they also concluded that these professionals, when promoted, performed poorly as managers, consequently imposing significant costs to the businesses analysed.

We tend to promote employees to management based on their previous, non-managerial, performance – not on their future managerial potential. This is a two-pronged problem. First, we end up with too many incompetent managers, of course. But second, these incompetent managers are likely to accept the promotion with a high self-confidence tied to competencies that are rendered invalid in a fundamentally new discipline. As such, they will never accumulate the humbleness and self-awareness needed to become not just efficient managers, but great leaders. In fact, they will never devote much time to reflect on why they even became managers and would not view their new-found responsibility as a calling, but as a mere position that they are entitled to based on their past performance. In the best-case scenario they become good managers, but never great leaders. And we need executives to be both if the desired outcome is meaningfulness for the employees under their responsibility.

Ultimately, managers are no more or less morally competent or incompetent than anybody else. First and foremost, they are people, and every human being has a sensitive streak. However, if we don't promote people to managers based on their managerial potential and the regime then demands the systematic pursuit of fixed targets, devoid of existential attention and ambitions, then instilling meaningfulness isn't exactly a priority. No manager has ever been promoted or rewarded for having raised their department's collective sense of meaning and self-awareness by 22%. But increase profitability or turnover by the same percentage and they can expect to be commended and praised, no matter how many people were exploited along the way. Managers do what they do because they've never been taught anything else, nor have they been expected to do anything else. The current generation of managers lack moral resonance. They simply aren't equipped to understand the need for a meaningful working environment for their staff or to provide it. The way in which we manage ourselves and others is morally incompetent, and that makes it existentially meaningless.

The way we manage, both at work and outside of it, does little to help modern human beings find meaning in the madness. In order to do so, management would have to be based on an entirely different starting point. Take, for example, the most common deathbed regret: working too much. This ought to give us pause for thought about whether our leadership is anchored in an ethical imperative, in a genuine desire to do good. That's not easy, especially if humanism is considered antithetical to capitalism. However, as Danish philosopher K.E. Løgstrup wrote in 1956, "What is demanded is that the demand should not have been necessary". In other words, if one 'did good' by default, a demand wouldn't be a necessary in the first place.[40]

The demand to do good arises from the clash of inclination and duty, selfishness and altruism. In the haste of our everyday lives, we have forgotten what leadership actually entails. This leaves us vulnerable to our basest inclinations. In such a situation, if that which is most important is not quantifiable, then that which is quantifiable rapidly becomes the most important. For example, if we only measure the speed at which we close units, reorganize teams and cut costs, we may tell ourselves that we've added value and been successful as a leader and manager. However, if we do not also evaluate whether the changes have been meaningful for those affected, then in the medium or long term, we will have irrevocably damaged organizational and human value.

Nothing is more important than ensuring that the work has meaning for those who do it. Here, too, Løgstrup imparts wisdom about management that very few McKinsey consultants will ever mention. He states that for every single person with whom you interact, you are responsible for a tiny piece of their life. "We never have something to do with another person without holding something of their life in our hands," he wrote. "It can be very little, a passing mood, a spiritedness withered or awakened, a loathing deepened or lifted. But it can also be terrifyingly great so that whether the other person's life flourishes or not is simply down to us."[41]

As a manager, you hold in your hands a relatively large slice of your employees' lives. You have a responsibility to ensure you do not make them sick and ideally that you help make their lives meaningful. With that in mind, what is the most significant way to evaluate the effect of your leadership? Surely it is to ensure that nobody will regret their time under your management. That would be no mean feat, especially in a world in which Human Resource Management and the compartmentalization of life are the norm. However, given that the prevailing management style is making so many people ill, we owe it to ourselves and each other to seek radical change.

A massive decade-long Swedish study[42] found that working for a bad manager was linked to an increase in incidents of unstable angina and heart attacks resulting in hospitalization or death. It also found a 50% increase in the risk of cardiovascular disease in employees exposed to psychosocially dysfunctional workplaces. In this context, poor management was defined as selfish, punitive and ill-tempered. Creeping dehumanization has slowly but surely driven a bigger and bigger wedge between managers and employees. There really is a pressing need to ensure that unethical tendencies aren't allowed to usurp our duty to do good.

Human beings are good at accumulating power but are not as good at turning it into something meaningful. This is one of the great paradoxes and challenges facing modern managers, or indeed, facing the concept of management itself. As the career-minded scamper ambitiously up the greasy pole, they accumulate more and more power and get better and better at using it to exploit human potential for financial and commercial gain. At the same time, however, they appear to lose their ability to use that same power to create a space in which individuals are able to realize their potential and make the most of the one life they have. The influence we exert on every single person in our network, especially as managers, is based on a mutual existential demand – the inevitable mutual responsibility that we have on each other for a full life.

LEADERSHIP AS A MUTUAL EXISTENTIAL DEMAND

According to a study,[43] 90% of all managers identify the inability to generate meaning as the single biggest impediment to high performance. Employees are experiencing a loss of meaning, and an entire generation of managers is struggling to tackle the problem.

It may seem alien to us as leaders, but we would nonetheless be wise to take this to heart, and approach it in the fact-based, structured and serious manner expected of us in the world of business. Only once creating meaning is considered as valuable as the organization or company's profitability will we see the necessary changes in behaviour. For those still not convinced, it should be sufficient to say that meaningfulness makes a better business tomorrow than the one we have today because it drives productivity, innovation and employee retention better than anything else. Nonetheless, the most important aspect is that nobody should end up regretting the one life they have lived because of the way they were managed at work. We should seize the opportunity to adopt this as the most important management key performance indicators (KPIs).

This assumes, of course, that the people for whom you are responsible are willing to be led. Part of the problem is that we've outsourced leadership to the managers. Leadership isn't performed at a distance, like salsa. It's more intimate, like a tango. The manager can only lead if the employees allow themselves to be led. Only in this way can we climb the ladder to self-respect.

If the way we're led is causing us more stress than it relieves, then the most obvious place to look for the root of the problem is the manager. Although there is much for which individual managers can and should be blamed, it's worth thinking more carefully about the relationship between manager and employee. The question is often whether we are good enough to manage. It isn't difficult to ascertain that we're not. However, instead of continually picking at this already sore point, it may be more interesting to ask ourselves and each other whether we're good enough at *being led* – and whether we've outsourced too much leadership to the managers.

It is not very fruitful to dig in and prepare for trench warfare between, on one side, managers and employers, eager to exploit, and on the other, employees and unions, calling for a separate private life, work-life balance and more time off. If we are to have any chance of seeing the light and gaining some wisdom before we retire, then employees must make just as much of an effort as managers. If we don't let ourselves and our self-awareness be led, no manager can do much to help us realize our human potential. Other people can't force us up the ladder of self-respect. Managers can show the way, but ultimately, we have to climb the rungs ourselves. Very few workplaces have 'Know thyself' carved into the office wall, but that shouldn't stop us seeking self-insight. A manager can only practise existential leadership if people allow themselves to be led.

Opening our minds and letting life into work and work into life is not without risk. Our managers are, in all probability, incapable of providing the existential leadership we need. They may be well-meaning Neanderthals with good hearts and the best of intentions, but they lack the requisite empathy, finesse or musicality to manage other people properly. Peeling off the Teflon coating is dangerous. As soon as we make ourselves existentially available to other people, but don't feel that our wellbeing and potential are being protected and developed, then we should turn our backs and walk away. But nor should we expect a fountain of meaning at work unless we are prepared to share what it is that we think would make our life meaningful. For an employer to support us and help us to protect and develop our self-worth and self-respect, we must first possess self-insight and self-awareness. This calls for us to recognize that meaning is best realized by the least possible distance and greatest possible intimacy.

4

PROFESSIONAL INTIMACY AND PLATONIC LOVE

PROFESSIONAL DISTANCE

A couple years ago, a Danish hospital sought to shed light on why work-related stress is so prevalent these days.[44] Hundreds of outpatients of the occupational health clinic were asked to identify the cause of their severe stress. Most named three or four work-related reasons, such as poor management, restructuring and excessive workloads, and a single private issue, usually divorce. Asked the same question, their employers only mentioned private matters, such as buying a new house, having twins or going through a divorce.

How can our interactions with each other be so hopelessly aloof, naïve and irresponsible that we don't at least acknowledge that the thing that occupies half of our employees' waking weekday hours has a significant influence on their psyche and wellbeing? Is it so inconceivable that there may be circumstances in the workplace that have triggered stress? Work is a highly intimate part of our lives. It has an enormous influence and, as such, has the potential to be dangerous in the wrong hands. Managers do indeed hold a large part of their employees' lives in their hands. This can be deadly – literally – if influence isn't exerted in the right way and for the right purposes.

One thing is certain: managers can't fulfil their responsibilities at a distance. In relationships, we can't take an existential starting point, a caring for each other, if we base them solely on the parts of our respective lives that overlap via work. Every employee lives one life, in one time, as one whole and complex person. If we're only interested in roughly a third of the person – and even then, maintain a professional distance from that third – it's no wonder that we give such embarrassingly wrong answers about the causes of stress among our staff.

It is simply impossible to gain insight into another person's sense of meaning in life (or lack thereof) if we adopt a professional distance from them. It is unprofessional, amateurish and irresponsible to distance ourselves from people for whom we have a significant responsibility.

Although it is impossible to specify exactly when the concept of professional distance emerged in management theory, it is relatively easy to imagine the kind of fossilized theorist back in the day who thought that management was most effective from afar. Unfortunately, this is often precisely the advice given to aspiring new managers as they don their new suits for the first time. We're told that it's important to keep a certain distance and go home early from office parties. Clearly, this advice is well-intentioned. Indeed, distancing is quite an effective technique if the idea is to justify to yourself the fact that yesterday's peers and colleagues are today's resources and subordinates. In that case, distance, Teflon and exploitation are absolutely the right strategy for avoiding post-promotion pangs of conscience in the transition from colleague to manager.

But since we know that intimacy and attending cultural events make by far the biggest contribution to our sense of wellbeing and meaning in life, should we not look at whether it is possible to incorporate intimacy and culture into the workplace to a greater extent? And no, it's not a matter of turning the workplace into a party zone.

In terms of philosophy, it is interesting that work, which is an intimate part of our lives, seems to be paradoxically devoid of intimacy. But as human beings, intimacy is precisely what we seek. It is the main ingredient in a meaningful life. We often regret not allowing ourselves to have been more intimate.

Not letting ourselves be happy. Not spending more time with the people we love. Not expressing our feelings more. Work isn't built up around expressing our innermost feelings and finding answers to the question of who we are. It cultivates neither our self-awareness nor our ability to find the meaning in life. Instead, it is a break from life – from real life. We've convinced ourselves and each other that this is fine because our lives are divided into something called 'working time' and something else called 'private time'. Work must not interfere with what you do in your own time and vice versa. When our lives are split, work becomes a break from life, and we don't subject it to the same existential demands and expectations. But it is also a break from everything that means anything to us, and we end up regretting it. The unpredictability of life has a habit of chipping away at our Teflon coating, at our self-confidence. Eventually, we find ourselves on our deathbeds, not knowing who we are and desperately wondering whether the life we have lived was the right one and dignified, whether we lived up to our human potential. Work is the first thing we regret. Why on Earth did we allow ourselves to live a third of our life starved of existential oxygen?

Is there any reason why work should be so sterile and ascetic? Do we really have to split our personality, our time and our lives for them to be bearable? Of course, we need limits and responsibilities, structures and obligations. But the language we use to express ourselves, and the way we manage or are managed, is a source of regret at best and often even of serious illness. So, what do we stand to lose by making space for intimacy in the professional world?

APOLLO AND DIONYSUS

When Nietzsche examined ancient Greek art, he applied the lens of two opposing forces, reflected in the gods Apollo and Dionysus. He extracted that the ancient Greeks had two conflicting attitudes to life, the Apollonian and the Dionysian, that when juxtaposed revealed some quite significant truths about our existence. Apollo represented asceticism, light and reason. His followers believed that our intellect would lead the way to an ethical life. The inscription at the entrance to the Temple of Apollo at Delphi said, 'Know thyself', but there was also another, lesser-known inscription: 'Nothing in excess'. This was a reminder that human beings can't expect to achieve the same good fortune and happiness as the gods. Our expectations of life shouldn't be too high; instead, we should submit to the conditions given to us. According to the Apollonian understanding of life, we must accept our mortal limitations and, in an ascetic manner, dutifully play our role in life so that we help to maintain order and harmony. To serve Apollo is to serve wisdom, rationality and limitation; essentially, it's to serve and cultivate professionalism. It is reason, intellect and moderation that win the day, while will and chaos are curbed and suppressed.

According to the ancient myths, when Apollo left the temple at summer's end, his half-brother Dionysus took over as the oracle for the winter. This is roughly equivalent to appointing Beelzebub as Pope. The Dionysian understanding of life contrasted sharply with the Apollonian. Dionysus, the god of wine and ecstasy, didn't let himself be tied down by reason. He sought intoxication, carnality and chaos. He was worshipped with orgies, festivals and plays, both tragedies and comedies. The aim was to let the suppressed sides of human nature bubble up to the surface, paying no heed to everyday constraints and inhibitions. To serve Dionysus is to serve the wild, the ecstatic and the limitless, to serve and worship the intimate. Wildness, enthusiasm and spontaneity are the order of the day, and any boundaries and structures are ignored.

In many ways, the Apollonian and the Dionysian represent different sides of the human psyche. On the one hand, a need for order and reason; on the other, an impulse toward wildness and intoxication. Culture versus nature. Civilization versus barbarism. Cosmos versus chaos. Weekday versus weekend. When it comes to our life, and therefore work, we need both elements to be present. If we serve only Apollo, the wise, the rational and the restrained, we will be professional all of the time. Without Dionysus, life is too ascetic and restrictive. Hierarchies and bureaucracy overshadow any form of will and emotion, and our workplace ends up being, as it does for so many people today, somewhere resistant to love – a place from which we maintain an existential distance. On the other hand, if we serve only Dionysus, the heady and ecstatic, we are only ever intimate. Without the moderating influence of Apollo, our impulses become so unrestrained as to be destructive. If work consists of nothing but orgies and religious festivals, it will be just a tad too volatile in the long term.

As Nietzsche concluded, neither of these two extremes can stand alone. They are part of a continuum and only make sense in relation to each other. In order for our lives to be meaningful, we must unite the Apollonian and the Dionysian. First, just as it is sometimes good to be restrained and orderly in our private lives, work must be capable of accommodating tragedy, comedy and intimacy. We do not need to choose between professionalism and intimacy – what we need is professional intimacy. We need a form of intimacy that accommodates our need to bear and express the most heartfelt sentiments, and our need to feel and give love, not just recognition or feedback. At the same time, we need a form of professionalism that recognizes the importance of rationality, while also making room for the basic human need for intimacy. Without this, there is no meaning. Without meaning, there is no productivity.

Second, professionalism can bring order and direction to intimacy, to ensure that the focus remains on achieving the organization's overall purpose. Even an Ancient Greek orgy required planning and structure to make it a success. Equally, meetings or workshops must be driven by a certain amount of vigour and drive if they are to be inspirational and energising.

In modern times, we make far greater sacrifices to Apollo than to Dionysus, and it really isn't all that surprising. We have quite simply inherited the idea, taken it on board and accustomed ourselves to believe that the correct ratio of professional to intimate is 5:2. Five weekdays of work, followed by two weekend days of life. We endure five days devoid of intimacy and ecstasy, during which we are unable to breathe properly, and then spend the weekend rehydrating the body and mind with love and energy. Often, we throw ourselves into a tightly-packed calendar of social events (akin to Dionysian festivals) from Friday evening until Sunday afternoon. The aim is to squeeze in as much life as possible before Monday morning, when we return to 'working life' to be exploited and burned out.

WHY YOU SHOULD LOVE YOUR BOSS – AND VICE VERSA

As managers, we have a professional duty that is also existential. We have a duty to manage in a way that attempts to create meaning and do so by creating professional intimacy, as opposed to professional distance. The workplace must also be a space in which love can take root. But what kind of love are we talking about? To answer this question, we must first understand that there are several types of love. When we talk about love, we usually think of romance and lust for a spouse or partner. We think of relationships and falling in love. We think of marriage, which we want to be more than just a practical arrangement, but something that will contribute to a lifelong sense of belonging and attraction.

The Ancient Greek philosophers had a different view of love. In his *Symposium*, Plato outlines a number of ideas about the nature of love. The literal translation of symposium is 'drinking party', and indeed, precisely such a gathering provided the setting for the text. In fact, it's the second day of the party, and several of the guests are hungover. They agree to take a break from the wine and send the women away so that they can entertain each other with a philosophical discussion about the nature of love, or *eros* – physical desire, sensual love, the reproductive urge, the insatiable appetite for more.

At first, they discuss the body, then the soul, and then the primacy of the spiritual relationship. Eventually, Socrates speaks.

He argues that *eros* is not directed at a person or soul, but at the underlying reason why we love somebody. He states that we are essentially in love with 'the good', which we experience first as a physical thing, for example in a beautiful body, but as we grow wiser, we increasingly find the good in thought – in the underlying, in what is beneath the surface.

As the symposium again turns somewhat Dionysian, some attendees party on, others leave or fall asleep. As readers, we are left pondering the assertion that love is more than just lust. Love can be directed at a friend, an idea or a purpose.

The Greeks employed a wide variety of concepts to describe love's many nuances and faces. Three of these are particularly significant: *agápe, storgé* and *philía. Agápe* is nonerotic love for a fellow human being. It is a self-sacrificing and self-devotional love, the universal love of the neighbour. *Storgé* is natural or instinctive love, for example, between children and parents. *Philiá*, however, describes an equal love between two people. It is a love of respect, of a deep and sincere friendship, a bond between soulmates – a bond based on love and friendship.

According to Aristotle, friends can be bound to each other in different ways – three, in fact. One of them is utility, i.e., it is beneficial to both parties. This type is temporary by definition. Once the utility value dries up, so does the friendship. Most of us have experienced this with work colleagues. You enjoy the time you spend together and provide each other with mutual benefit, but as soon as the situation changes, the relationship often changes quite significantly. Many of us have had a good and trusted colleague whose company we enjoyed, but with whom we have had very little or nothing to do since the end of the working relationship.

The second type of friendship, which also arises more or less accidentally, is characterized by temporary enjoyment or satisfaction. It is more emotional than the first type and often emerges between classmates or teammates. It too is short-lived, as it tends to stop if the situation or preferences change. Many young people go through different phases in which they explore a range of interests. As they do so, the gallery of characters changes as well.

Many friendships fall into one of these two categories, which are more or less determined by happenstance. The same also applies to working relationships. Many of these fall into the first category, as they usually involve a mutually beneficial exchange. Some fall into the second, for those fortunate enough to be working together on something of mutual interest.

The higher form of friendship known as *philía* involves no mutual utility or temporary pleasure. This form of friendship is much more profound and more fundamental. It is a relationship and a friendship based to a greater extent on a love of the ethics and the purpose of life that the other person epitomizes and aspires to. The other person is viewed as an end in themselves, rather than as a source of utility or enjoyment. The relationship will continue even if there is no mutual benefit or exchange of pleasure. This is a friendly love that is not incidental or based on a particular situation but on the other person's virtues. In other words, it is a love of the fundamental nature of the other but – in line with Plato's bacchanal festivities – also of the meaning behind those virtues and the direction in which they point. It is a love of the primary purpose that drives the other person, of something we can never quite grasp purely intellectually.

It is best described by Michel de Montaigne in his essay "Friendship," where he concludes that he loves his friend Etienne de La Boétie so deeply: "because it was he, because it was I." Or as Astrid Lindgren puts it in a divine moment in one of the Emil of Lönneberga books,[45] when the titular character says, "You and I, Alfred." Alfred replies, "Yes, you and I, Emil." This is the most masterful encapsulation of the nature of friendship. So simple, so uncomplicated, so close and so deep.

For most of us, love between colleagues is usually synonymous with an affair at the office Christmas party. However, I contend that there is another form of love in the workplace, one that is professionally fruitful. It is my sincere belief that any professional relationship should ultimately be based on platonic love between two individuals. This love is not unrestrained love based on lust. It is a bond that starts and ends with a love of the virtues and the purpose around which the relationship revolves. When you share so much of your one life with your workplace and your colleagues and when, as a manager, you hold an important part of your employees' lives in your hands, you have a duty to treat these lives with the same respect and love with which you treat your own and any other life that you encounter.

Basically, this type of relationship requires a necessary degree of goodness, decency and generosity from each party to get off the ground. Those who lack empathy or don't care for others will seldom enter into such relationships. They will only seek relationships based on utility or pleasure. By entering into the third kind of friendship and *philía*, we also paradoxically achieve the benefits of the other two – utility and pleasure are automatically included. But this calls for intimacy.

You need to see the other party as a whole person. If we acknowledge that we live one life, in one time, as one person, should we not apply the same ambitions to our working relationships as we do to other parts of our lives? Should we not be consistent and set the bar at the same height? Why not strive for *philía* with your boss or with the employees for whom you are responsible?

One could argue against this by referring to the inherent asymmetry in the relation between boss and employee, as the former holds the power to trigger a termination of the latter's employment. Why risk to indulge yourself in a relation with a boss with little or no control over its reciprocity or duration? First, the idea that we can enjoy absolute equality in any relation is absurd. Whether between colleagues, spouses, friends or lovers there will never be a state of complete equilibrium. Equality is derived from the mathematical world, describing when two entities weigh exactly the same or have exactly the same length. In our practical, human world, we cannot always love each other *exactly* the same and the one is never *exactly* as dependent on the other as vice versa. The parties are never equally powerful, beautiful or intelligent. Second, any relation is based on faith. We take a risk when we indulge our body and mind to the other. The risk of failure, the risk of wasting our potential, even our love. But any risk taken with a hint of rationality entails the opportunity of a corresponding reward. And if we acknowledge the possibility that somewhere out there, in the labour market, there exists a boss that would return our faith and lead us with empathy and love, it makes little sense not to manoeuvre our way towards that person. For me, the risk of not doing it significantly outweighs the risk of failing at it.

All of this requires a recruitment process that emphasizes character, ethics and virtues rather than grades, credits or skills. Grades and credits are akin to money, in that their value is determined by how they are earned and achieved. If grades or credits are earned in a way that diminishes your humanity – and therefore self-awareness – they are of lesser value. In other words, the starting point for recruitment should be a sincere sensitivity to – indeed, a love for – the potential appointee. There must be a recognition of or at least curiosity about whether there is an overlap between your purpose in life and theirs. It is this mutual ethical demand that endows the relationship with an existential starting point, rather than an operational one, and makes the path to a meaningful life, as opposed to a satisfied or happy one, shorter.

THE GREEKS EMPLOYED A WIDE VARIETY
OF CONCEPTS TO DESCRIBE LOVE'S MANY
NUANCES AND FACES. THREE OF THESE
ARE PARTICULARLY SIGNIFICANT:
AGÁPE, STORGÉ AND PHILÍA.

AGÁPE IS NONEROTIC LOVE FOR A FELLOW
HUMAN BEING. IT IS A SELF-SACRIFICING
AND SELF-DEVOTIONAL LOVE, THE
UNIVERSAL LOVE OF
THE NEIGHBOUR.

STORGÉ IS NATURAL OR INSTINCTIVE
LOVE, FOR EXAMPLE, BETWEEN
CHILDREN AND PARENTS.

PHILÍA, HOWEVER, DESCRIBES AN
EQUAL LOVE BETWEEN TWO PEOPLE.
IT IS A LOVE OF RESPECT, OF A DEEP AND
SINCERE FRIENDSHIP, A BOND BETWEEN
SOULMATES – A BOND BASED ON
LOVE AND FRIENDSHIP.

5

MEANINGFUL
LEADERSHIP

IQ vs EQ vs MQ

On 7 May 1915, a German U-boat torpedoed and sank a British passenger ship off the coast of Ireland. Almost 1,200 passengers died en route from Liverpool to New York, including 128 Americans. At the time, the United States was maintaining a neutral stance on the war that was raging in Europe. Despite growing calls for revenge from the American people, President Woodrow Wilson bit his lip hard and counselled diplomacy instead of war. Only after the loss of a further seven US merchant ships and the interception of a telegram outlining Germany's intention to support a Mexican invasion of the southern US, did Wilson finally declare war on Germany in spring 1917.

At the time, the American army mustered a mere 300,000 or so men, a paltry number compared with the 11-million-strong German army. This prompted the US government to conscript 2.8 million men aged 18–45. Even though the urgency of the situation meant that the bar was set low, there was still a need to evaluate which of the conscripts or volunteers were actually suitable to serve, and if so, where and how. The sudden demand for millions of new recruits presented a challenge to the administration's ability to verify and classify the recruits for various military roles effectively. This required an intelligence test to be administered on a scale never before seen and psychologists were summoned to develop one. During the war, almost two million American recruits were tested on subjects like maths, logic and general knowledge to determine whether they were fit to serve, which jobs would suit them best and to identify those who would make good officers. Despite its horrors and barbarism, the war paved the way for a practical breakthrough in psychology, because it offered an opportunity to field-test theories about intelligence testing on a massive scale. After the war, it was significantly easier for psychology to attract funding and recognition, as it had proved its worth in a highly practical and visible manner.

German psychologist and philosopher Ludwig Wilhelm Stern pioneered a system based on logic tests that calculated the subject's mental age, which was then divided by their real age and multiplied by 100. He called the result the 'Intelligence Quotient' or 'IQ'. If someone's mental age is the same as their real age, their IQ is 100.

IQ testing has subsequently become by far the most studied and widely used method of measuring human intelligence. Since its introduction during World War I, it has found its way into all sorts of educational institutions and workplaces and is still the predominant indicator of intelligence. Indeed, it is hard to avoid these kinds of tests, which are used as part of admission to higher education and in recruitment and appointment processes. However, even during World War I, questions were asked about whether they were a reliable way to measure an individual's abilities. How intelligent are intelligence tests? How can we measure something as abstract as a person's intelligence in the first place, let alone express it in just a single number?

With millions of potential recruits and hundreds of job applicants out there, it is convenient and efficient to use a simple test or a GPA to separate the sheep from the herd and focus on identifying the best candidate. However, 'best' here refers to those who have mastered one specific type of intelligence – an intelligence that primarily describes the ability to think logically. The success of this unit of measurement has meant that we have traditionally looked for and sought to motivate staff in knowledge-based jobs based on what IQ represents. In other words, these cognitive skills have become the gold standard for success in life. Ultimately, we get what we measure. When we know that the probability of achieving what we want rises if we master a particular skill, then we will focus on mastering it, be it mental arithmetic or one-handed clapping. If problem-solving skills are at the top of the employers' shopping list – which, according to the World Economic Forum, they are and still will be in 2022[46] – then those are precisely what potential employees will seek to acquire or develop.

What the labour market expects of us quickly becomes what we also expect from the labour market – to be intellectually stimulated. Traditionally, training in companies and organizations has been a matter of supporting professional and technical development and learning. It is about providing the staff with intellectual stimulus because that is primarily what employees are expected to glean from their work. This includes access to knowledge and resources, as well as clarity about objectives, roles and expectations.

Physics genius Albert Einstein supposedly never took an intelligence test. At least, there is no evidence of him ever doing so. However, given that he was a Nobel Prize-winning scientist whose work formed the basis for our very understanding of the universe, it is reasonable to assume that he probably had an IQ well above average. Nonetheless, he had a more nuanced understanding of intelligence than the one expressed in the World War I recruitment tests. Einstein said, "If you want your children to be intelligent, read them fairy tales. If you want them to be more intelligent, read them more fairy tales."[47] He also thought that the primary measuring unit for intelligence should be the ability to change and develop.

The most important sign of intelligence is, therefore, neither logic nor knowledge, but imagination.

However, in the job market of today, if you want to be attractive to employers, it's no longer enough just to be intellectually stimulated or intelligent, at least not in a one-dimensional, cognitive sense. According to the World Economic Forum[48] and based on input from HR and strategy executives from the world's leading companies, traits such as 'creativity' and 'emotional intelligence' have recently entered the top ten most sought-after employee characteristics. They are expected to remain there in 2022. We have long since paved the way for a different understanding of intelligence, including by using the concept of emotional intelligence.

Emotional Quotient (EQ) is the ability to understand, deal with and navigate your own and other people's emotions. It places much greater emphasis on intelligence in relation to self-awareness, cooperation and empathy. Via EQ, we begin to articulate work as something that creates identity, something to which we are also emotionally and socially connected. This makes EQ an important tool and character trait for the modern manager, who deploys it to stimulate this need, which in many ways resembles a craving for happiness. Work is now supposed to be a source of experiences, relationships and a sense of belonging. It isn't supposed just to lead to development and stimulation on a technical and professional level, but also strike emotional and personal chords.

In 1977, Abraham Zaleznik drew his distinction between management and leadership. This was an example of a break with IQ-based thinking and a movement toward a more social or emotional understanding of success and intelligence.

A second and at least equally controversial breakthrough came in 1983 when Harvard professor Howard Gardner published his theory of multiple intelligences.[49] He challenged the traditional approach to measuring intelligence and called for a far more nuanced understanding. For example, was Einstein really more intelligent than Michael Jordan? In the academic sense, yes. But Einstein would most likely fare poorly if he were asked to weave his way through a defence and pass the ball to an unmarked teammate. Intelligence must, therefore, come in many different shapes and sizes – eight, to be precise. In addition to logical/mathematical intelligence, Gardner also identified linguistic intelligence, musical intelligence, bodily intelligence, visual intelligence, interpersonal intelligence, intra-personnel intelligence and naturalistic intelligence.

He later flirted with the idea of adding a ninth: existential intelligence, to describe the ability to reflect upon the meaning of life. While Gardner remains unconvinced of the necessity for existential intelligence, one of the world's leading and most dogged advocates of IQ is a convert. In 2013, consulting firm McKinsey added Meaning Quotient (MQ) to IQ and EQ, hailing it as the best way to motivate staff to go the extra mile.[50] They argued that current and future generations will expect their work to help them find a sense of meaning in life to a higher degree than ever before and that is, to put it mildly, exactly what the world needs. The most important character trait a manager can possess is not IQ or EQ, but MQ – the ability to help others to find a sense of meaning in life through the work they do.

That is not to suggest that we should throw cognitive stimulation or emotional understanding under the bus, but nor has our former reverence for them – either separately or together – taken us to the destination promised when we paid our fare. Instead, we need the kind of intelligence, musicality and dexterity that only MQ provides.

MEANINGFULNESS QUOTIENT (MQ)

We need to make fundamental changes in the way we lead and realize human potential. We also need to systematize and quantify meaningfulness as an essential parameter for both the management we provide and the life we live. Neither IQ nor EQ is enough, but what lies behind MQ? Let's start with a quick question. Who has the most meaningful work: an energy trader, who sits behind a computer screen every day, buying all sorts of energy to sell for a profit, or an aid worker who spends every day taking supplies to starving people in North Africa?

Somewhat surprisingly, the answer is the former, at least if we accept the results of the analysis that my colleagues and I conducted in 2016.[51] We found that the energy trading company Danish Commodities had a higher MQ than a group of NGO aid workers. How is that possible? To find the answer, we must first fully understand the nature of the MQ.

Many readers will object that meaning is entirely subjective – and they are, of course, correct. All emotions are subjective. Nonetheless, when we look at all of the subjective feelings that make work meaningful, a clear pattern emerges. Following an extensive literature review of scientific articles and studies, my research consultancy, Voluntas, boiled MQ down to four main ingredients that are the primary drivers for a sense of meaning in work. Purpose, belonging, personal growth and leadership combine to make a potent potion with which to conjure up the most fertile possible conditions for meaningfulness to germinate in the workplace.

PURPOSE

The first driver is a strong purpose – i.e., a clear idea of the difference the organization wants to make in the world.

How many organizations have been around for about 2,000 years and retain a 'customer base' of approximately two billion people? It is perhaps a bit unfair to compare a religious denomination with a commercial company, and the Vatican can serve as a poor example on many dimensions, but every business owner and entrepreneur should study the Roman Catholic Church and the Vatican as a form of senior management. The Catholic Church is more than just a religion. It is a global organization that has managed to maintain its relevance over several centuries.

The role of the Vatican is not very different from that of the senior management of a company. Every day, it has to produce a yield, albeit an existential one, in the form of making adherents continue to see and feel that being a Catholic is meaningful. And it has been eminently successful in this endeavour. But how is it done? First of all, the purpose of the Vatican extends far beyond just filling its own coffers. Quite simply, it has managed to keep Catholicism relevant to individuals throughout countless social changes over hundreds of years. The Church is not run on the basis of the bottom line, but on an existential demand that it should always add meaning to the life of every Catholic. If it failed to do so, there would be no more Catholics.

Companies and organizations should organize along similar lines – around a purpose that, in terms of both ambition and timescale, extends far beyond the next quarterly report. As managers, especially as senior executives or owners, we must ask ourselves, "What is the point? Why do we exist? For whom do we make a difference?" It is just as important for a company as it is for an individual to be able to reply when someone asks, "Who are you?"

Filling the shareholders' pockets isn't enough. Any organization that wants to be an attractive workplace in the future should take its purpose seriously.

A study by Deloitte[52] showed that no fewer than 70% of millennials who responded expect employers to focus on solving social problems. In fact, half of them said that they would rather work for a company with a purpose than earn a higher salary. Of course, earning money is still essential. It is a prerequisite, a necessity. It is the oxygen of business. Without it, a company simply cannot breathe. But breathing should never be an end in itself unless our sole ambition is to live a life that is completely uninspiring, insignificant, without hope – in other words, meaningless. Without revenue, a company will not survive, no matter how admirable its purpose. But the single-minded pursuit of profit is not really an aim worth striving for and is far from sustainable in the longer term. It is certainly isn't what has kept the Vatican alive and relevant at the top of the Catholic Church century after century.

A clear purpose gives every manager a North Star by which to navigate. Communicating it clearly to the staff makes their work meaningful. It injects energy and direction into our work when we understand the difference we are making, a difference that goes beyond the mere functional content of our day-to-day duties.

For employees to feel this way, it is crucial that management formulates and communicates the organization's purpose in a way that is readily understood. It should also be reflected in our daily work. If it is not, then the purpose will not ring true and the staff may even deride it as just a marketing stunt.

I saw for myself how meaningful it can be to have a clear purpose when, in 2012 and 2013, Vestas, one of the biggest wind turbine manufacturers in the world, faced the worst crisis in its history. We announced 6,500 redundancies, approximately one-third of the workforce. In other words, we created a reality in which the staff on the shop floor were not sure if they would have a job the next day, or if the company would survive, or be snapped up by overseas investors.

Like any other self-respecting global organization, we measured everything it was possible to quantify. Given the circumstances, there was little enthusiasm for this process, but one thing surprised me: although we sacked people, and then sacked more, and then even more, those that were left continued to display a sense of duty and a strong work ethic. In fact, the upheaval appeared to make no difference to the quality of their work. Quite simply, they worked just as hard and as well as ever. We asked if it was because they had confidence in the company's strategy, but they said no. In fact, very few actually knew what the strategy was. When we asked if it was because they had confidence in the management, 'no' was again the polite version of the answer.

This piqued my curiosity. In a period so barbaric, uncertain and by any measure meaningless, why did they remain loyal and hard-working? Two things stood out.

One was that they considered the product extremely mean-ingful. Vestas' *purpose* – to help change the world's energy mix and combat climate change by providing wind technology – gave them a sense of meaning in life. They felt that they were part of something larger and that their work directly contributed to solving one of the biggest challenges facing our planet. They may not have been familiar with the company strategy and may even have trusted the local used car dealer more than their own management, but they knew that their work was ultimately important. Given that meaning was clearly so important to the staff, this realization made me reflect on whether the management had been running the company in a way that made the Vestas purpose clear at all times.

The second element was the employees' sense of *belonging* with their colleagues. In other words, they turned up to work for *each other*, not for the shareholders or the management. This made me reflect further on whether management had done enough to promote a social community and platonic love between colleagues.

BELONGING

The sense of belonging with other people is an integral part of our experience of meaningfulness. When we acknowledge that life cannot be split or divided, we must also acknowledge the importance of others understanding and accepting us as we are – not just as a colleague, parent or employee, but as a human being.

Social relations born out of mutual recognition of each other as people are therefore an important consideration for managers. We must take extremely seriously our responsibility to cocreate and support social communities. This is not to say that a manager should buy foosball tables and bring in cake every Wednesday. Indeed, far from it. Fringe benefits like those only bring momentary satisfaction, and it's not the primary task of a manager to provide fleeting happiness. Instead, it is a matter of setting a good example, of embodying honest, respectful and inquisitive conduct, and creating a working environment in which employees are able to get to know one another. This is the type of environment that creates fertile ground for relationships that extend beyond the purely professional, as well as for communities based on equality and intimacy, in which each member can safely say what they can and cannot do, and what they think and believe. In a space like that, even a seemingly unexceptional group of people can produce the most impressive ideas and results.

It is important to stress that, as a driver for work-related meaningfulness, a sense of belonging is not just about fitting neatly, perfectly and immediately into a given context from day one, like the missing piece in a jigsaw. It is just as much about experiencing a convergence between your values and virtues and those to which the company aspires – in other words, the workplace's worldview and basic ideals being in harmony with your own.

As managers, we should work to establish communities that exhibit the characteristics mentioned above. In this context, it is absolutely imperative that managers are not only capable of making clear and complying with the organization's virtues, but also ensuring that the employees feel that they have a role to play, that they mean something to others and that they are contributing to the community.

A company like Joe & The Juice, one of the fastest-growing Nordic retail brands, is a shining example of how to create a strong sense of belonging between employees and their workplace. What appears from the outside to be nothing more than a noisy juice bar is actually a vibrant community of young people that transcends economic, cultural, geographical and ethnic boundaries. I must declare a rather extreme vested interest here, as I have had the privilege of serving the company as vice chair since 2016. However, that role has granted me access to every nook and cranny of the company. I've seen for myself how the company has built its success, with thousands of employees in hundreds of locations.

The company's manifesto states, "We strive to develop a culture that delivers an unprecedented level of meaningfulness in the interface between our people and our workplace." These words have been brought to vivid life. Over the years, the company has largely been organized around its employees, instead of vice versa. This means, in practice, that all members of senior management, with one exception, are recruited internally. Almost everybody started their career behind a juice extractor and has been given the opportunity to grow and develop with the company. The company's main raw material is not freshly squeezed juice or loud music, but human potential. It has opened new branches in several locations and gives employees plenty of opportunities to explore interesting places outside work. The company has also invested in houses and apartment buildings so that staff working far from home can live under the same roof. Its internal training programme makes it possible for young people who don't do well in an IQ-centred learning environment to acquire knowledge and skills that make them employable and give them hope. When hiring and promoting people, technical skills are secondary; the company's first priority is the candidate's attitude.

Joe & The Juice is *also* built on elbow grease and efficient supply chains. However, it is the company's existential immune system that has enabled it to grow by nearly 50% p.a. over the last decade without compromising its culture. This has been possible because every decision is based on the objective of stimulating the social community between employees as much as possible. The thinking is that if our employees find it meaningful to work with each other, then this will be reflected in our turnover. The latter is a secondary effect of a fierce focus on the former, not vice versa.

PERSONAL GROWTH

The third of the four primary drivers of work-related meaningfulness is personal growth. In 2015, a group of researchers from the Université de Montréal conducted a survey[53] of the self-help books to which we increasingly turn. Do these books actually improve our lives? The researchers divided 30 subjects into two groups. Half avidly read self-help books; the other half did not. The group who read self-help literature performed markedly worse on all health parameters (stress level, self-discipline and tolerance). This suggests that effectively turning work into one big self-help book is a bad idea. However, the increasing popularity of self-help literature indicates that we are seeking guidance like never before, and the more instructive, the better.

So why are working people spending more and more of their leisure time reading these books? The answer seems obvious.

Work gives us a wage, a computer, maybe even fresh fruit, but not necessarily personal development. To create a sense of meaning in life, our work must not only provide access to a social community that we care about and an organizational purpose that we are proud to work toward, but also make us feel that every day we learn a little more about ourselves, our capabilities and our surroundings.

What meaning does your life have if every moment at work moves you further away from understanding and realizing your potential?

Far too many workplaces have a tendency to equate development with an endless list of in-service training and upskilling options. However, if we are to manage on the basis of meaningfulness, and on the premise that we only live one life, then we must also rethink the idea of staff development. It is vital that we focus on both professional and personal development – in other words, we must transition from staff development to realizing human potential. As a manager, your primary success criterion must be that you are able to help your staff better understand their strengths, weaknesses and, in particular, their potential, and support their growth on that basis. In other words, we must help them develop self-awareness, which leads to self-respect.

All too often, staff development focuses on climbing the greasy career pole as fast as possible, rather than patiently ascending the ladder of self-respect. This paradigm constantly encourages us to learn new technical skills, rather than get to know ourselves and live with the greatest possible dignity and meaning every day, no matter whether we are a company receptionist or a primary school teacher. But what's the rush, especially for young adults? We are living longer than ever before, and we are going to have to work longer than previous generations.

So relax, there's plenty of time to realize our professional and technical ambitions. However, the fact that we will have to work for what seems like forever makes it more important to get to grips with the existential dimensions of our lives as early as possible. It is precisely these tools – far more than any book on self-hypnosis or countless courses in accounting and finance – that will help you navigate life.

Horsens Council in Denmark has taken a progressive step. Its Department of Disability, Mental Health and Social Vulnerability now uses MQ to guarantee a holistic focus on its 500 employees. Its core purpose is to help local people with psychological, physical and/or social problems live a life that reflects their needs, dreams, hopes and goals. In order to provide this kind of support to the public, the council must reflect the same view of human nature internally. In simple terms, Horsens Council aims to help both its staff and the population of 100,000 in and around the city to achieve their human potential.

I have observed this process from the sidelines, and it has been highly instructive for all involved. At first, the focus was on the MQ of the managers in the department, and then on how we make work as meaningful as possible for employees of the council. This evolutionary journey has only been possible because senior management included people who realized that we only live one life, in one time, as one person. Having reached this conclusion, they then dared to ask themselves and each other how to make the time spent at work as meaningful as possible.

LEADERSHIP

The final driver of meaningfulness at work is leadership. Leadership should be understood slightly differently than the previous drivers. Management based on meaningfulness is primarily about creating frameworks for the other three drivers. This is because people who find a high degree of meaning in their work don't directly associate it with the specific actions of their manager. In other words, there is no evidence that a manager can *create* meaningfulness for an employee per se, just the *frameworks* that facilitate it. However, it is evident that managers must avoid creating *meaninglessness*. Several common leadership pitfalls will engender feelings of meaninglessness in members of staff. These include unfair treatment, taking employees for granted or isolating them.

To avoid these pitfalls, any management that takes itself and meaningfulness seriously must focus on creating frameworks that help staff understand the organization's purpose, foster a sense of belonging and make them feel they are developing as human beings.

The important thing is to develop managers who can create these frameworks, who can lead and act in accordance with the organization's purpose and clarify both the individual's contribution to their department and the department's contribution to the organization's overall objectives.

It is important to clarify these questions because a purpose, a sense of belonging and personal growth are not in themselves enough to create meaningfulness. For example, imagine being employed in an organization that has a purpose with which you very much identify, but where your day-to-day experience is that management is only interested in the bottom line, never the purpose. In other words, the management itself is inhibiting the employee's opportunities to derive meaning from the organization's purpose. While each individual has, to a great extent, the opportunity to shape their own lives, managers must be aware of the responsibility that comes with being in charge of the many decisions that can affect not only the employees' job and livelihood, but their overall quality of life. The workplace is not a democratic space in which individuals are free to shape their own conditions. The management sets the framework. In other words, the employees are crew members, but it is management that captains the ship and steers it into port. It is the responsibility of managers to create frameworks for the three other drivers.

No one is exempt from the need for meaningfulness. Nor does it arise by itself, as Danske Commodities, one of Europe's biggest energy trading companies, found out the hard way. Seen from the outside, this energy trading company appears to be an entrepreneurial utopia. As European countries liberalized energy trading, the company began trading across borders. Its business model involves buying energy at a low price in one country and selling it in another. Since 2004, solid business acumen has created hundreds of jobs and generated revenue in the billions.

In 2014, however, its fortunes changed dramatically, leading to a quarter of the staff being laid off. By 2015, things were turning around financially and the company was on the rise again, achieving the third best result in its history. Nonetheless, the management was perturbed. Although the company was again a resounding success and growing at a faster pace than ever before, something didn't feel quite right. Approximately one in five employees left the company of their own accord in 2015, including valued employees who the management wanted to keep. The financial turbulence was then followed by a period of cultural turmoil. What was missing was a leadership based on a strong and honest narrative about the company, which could steer the staff in the same direction and provide a perspective that extended beyond mere day-to-day duties. The basic pillar in the company's cultural revival was the development of a strategic narrative. It wrote a manifesto linking together the company's history, experiences, ideology and virtues. This united the organization – from the boardroom to the reception desk – around a single meaningful narrative about where Danske Commodities came from and where it was headed. It gave the employees a much clearer purpose, enshrined a more uniform worldview among management and described the culture and community on which the organization should be built. The company stopped losing staff, returned to the top of the 'Great Place to Work' rankings[54] and has posted the best results in its history. Had management focused solely on financial key data, they would never have noticed the cracks appearing in the company's cultural foundation and the story of Danske Commodities would have been completely different.

It is these four essential ingredients – purpose, personal growth, belonging and leadership – that drive a sense of meaning at work. This explains why aid workers don't necessarily feel that their jobs are more meaningful than the trader who spends every day selling energy for profit. Meaning is not determined by the type of business or industry in which we work, as all types of job have the potential to be meaningful. It is entirely a question of being aware of that fact and of whether the four pillars promote or prevent meaning in the individual's life.

In purely ethical terms, the aid workers' purpose is undoubtedly more worthy. Food aid keeps millions of people alive. But if the purpose is bogged down in a sense of hopelessness, if the leadership isn't purposeful, if we don't feel part of a social community and if we don't feel we are making any progress, then even the most virtuous cause may in practice find it difficult to generate meaning.

PERFORMANCE MANAGEMENT 2.0: THE MQ ANALYSIS

Nowadays, organizations measure virtually everything. Every single strategic and commercially important resource is measured and weighed to ensure it is fit for purpose and naturally, the same applies to the staff. Indeed, quantifying employees' welfare – be it wellbeing, satisfaction or commitment – is a lucrative business. Questionnaires, studies and employee feedback enable management to quantify the atmosphere 'on the shop floor' and navigate accordingly.

In Denmark, wellbeing assessments and the very idea of wellbeing at work were conceived in the 1960s during an economic boom. The sky-high employment levels at that time meant companies had to compete for labour. It was also during this period that concepts like job content and job satisfaction entered our vocabulary. Work had to be more than mere coercion and external demands. Wellbeing came to be understood as the fulfilment of employee expectations – if they are met, the employee will be satisfied. Perceptions of what precisely constitutes wellbeing have emphasized different aspects over the years, but this core concept remains largely unchanged.

This leaves us with two simple choices: either optimize working conditions, such as wages and hours, or lower the employee's expectations of their work.

Similarly, in an international context, the Chartered Institute of Personnel and Development has been assessing wellbeing in the workplace for more than 18 years.[55] There is an increasing focus on wellbeing and culture in the workplace and yet we struggle to answer why so many of us succumb to work-related stress. This gives rise to two possible conclusions: either we are measuring the wrong things, or the results generated are as much use as a chocolate teapot.

MQ is no panacea, but if meaningfulness demonstrably provides a more accurate picture of how an organization performs, both in commercial and human existential terms, and if the conclusion is that we can measure meaningfulness just as accurately as anything else, then why would we not measure it? Since meaningfulness is so important to innovation, productivity, commitment, retention and quality of life, it's a mystery that we expend so many resources on measuring just about everything else, none of which is as important in either human or business terms.

These days, it's more the rule than the exception to ask employees to wade through 60–70 interminable questions every six months. It then takes three months for the results to be analysed and translated into specific actions, the effectiveness of which is ultimately dubious at best. Management receives a whopper of a report with far more statistics than insights. And the delay between the feedback process and any changes being implemented is often so long that in the meantime the employees have lost hope or have even moved on.

If an organization relies heavily on a bunch of enthusiastic, hard-working people bursting through the door every morning and giving it their all, then nothing is more important than knowing whether their efforts create a sense of meaning for them. It is considered permissible to squeeze employees hard, as long as there is a two-way existential exchange. Managers should really toss and turn at night worrying about this far more than about whether market share is up or down 2%. But in truth, there's no need for sleepless nights. It is merely a matter of finding out whether your organization's MQ is up or down, and then identifying which managers excel at promoting MQ and those who need further intensive training or even help to find new jobs. Even a relatively obscure and semi-philosophical indicator like MQ can be measured just as digitally and efficiently as any other indicator. This may entail asking far fewer questions, but asking them more often, in order to track the progress of the organization's MQ, intervene at short notice if necessary and quickly observe the effect of the intervention in both human and financial terms.

The measurements are based on MQ's four main parameters:

1. Whether employees are familiar with and believe in the organization's purpose
2. Whether employees feel that they are growing
3. Whether employees feel an emotional and social sense of belonging with the other people in the organization
4. Whether employees feel that the leadership is both clear and human

Forget about other indicators. If the employees feel an underlying sense of meaning in life with the work they do every day, managers can sleep soundly. As long as managers make a significant contribution to realizing the human potential in an organization, the staff will remain loyal through thick and thin.

The most important lesson we can take from Harvard professor Howard Gardner is not the precise number of different intelligences, but that intelligence, more than anything else, is a skill we can train and develop. The same is true of MQ. It would be unreasonable to expect managers trained in IQ and EQ to become world champions in MQ overnight, but they will soon learn, provided we train them in it, emphasize its value and celebrate its use as an internal KPI. Even those with a natural talent – in music, mathematics or sport – need to practise and develop. All of us, managers and employees included, have untapped potential. Triggering this potential starts with the realization that every HR department should be abolished or at least renamed the Human Potential Leadership (HPL) department.

FROM HUMAN RESOURCE MANAGEMENT TO HUMAN POTENTIAL LEADERSHIP

Meaningful leadership is primarily about leading people on the basis of their potential, rather than managing them as resources. The idea is to lead in a way that helps individuals realize their potential, develop healthy self-awareness and be the best version of themselves.

When we talk about potential, what are we actually talking about? The potential to run 100 metres in under 10 seconds? The potential to be a scientist, entrepreneur, nurse or prime minister? Not really. None of these constitute essential aspects of human potential. The point is that everybody with cognitive skills has the potential to define and redefine the meaning of their lives continually by climbing the ladder of self-respect every day. Based on insight and awareness of the meaning of your life today, you can lead yourself toward living a more meaningful life tomorrow. Everybody is born with this ability, but they can only activate their life potential if they are aware they have it and feel personally obligated to realize it. Only then will they begin to insist on helping both themselves and each other climb the ladder of self-respect every day for the rest of their lives.

Potential should not be misinterpreted as an incentivizing trick, like a carrot that is constantly dangled 20 centimetres in front of our noses, no matter how fast we run. That kind of management would be devastating, because we don't know where the ceiling is until we hit it. Nor can potential be quantified. It makes no sense to say that our potential is 19 and today we are only at 17. It is more a question of identifying and trying to realize the purpose of our lives. We know who we want to be and who we don't want to be. We define our potential ourselves, informed and challenged by the people around us.

FLEXIBILITY AT WORK IS THE KEY, NOT BALANCE BETWEEN LIFE AND WORK

Meaningful leadership involves rejecting the idea of work-life balance and nurturing flexibility instead. There is no balance between life and work. At most, there is an imbalance. Ultimately, it's all just life, whether we spend it on work, sport, love or something else. Life should absorb work and subordinate it to our purpose. We should constantly measure and weigh work to determine whether it helps us realize our potential. In other words, does it increase or decrease our MQ?

Meaningful leadership is about flexibility. It is about embracing and planning around the fact that employees live and breathe 24 hours a day and aren't necessarily at their best between the hours of nine and five. According to Gallup's State of the American Workplace Report,[56] leaders should weave an element of flexibility into their culture in order to be competitive when it comes to recruitment. Sixty-three per cent of millennials say that they would be inclined to change jobs for flexible hours.

Once we recognize the intimate and existential nature of work, it is no longer something that is restricted to a particular place or skill. When work is no longer the opposite of life but is part of it, both employees and managers are more inclined to be flexible. If there is an overlap between our own individual purpose in life and that of our employer, we will go the extra mile, because it has meaning. If it has no meaning, we will either not do it or regret doing it, because we wasted valuable time from our one life without any existential return. Conversely, if we mutually acknowledge that work is existential, then employers should be more willing to be flexible. Partly because it will, in purely cynical terms, make it more likely that staff will stay with the company for longer, and partly (even primarily) because it reduces the probability that individuals will regret the time spent in that particular workplace.

All of this requires planning and trust, but if the relationship is built on a mutual existential demand, it is definitely achievable.

THE MEANINGFULNESS CONVERSATION

As soon as a manager acknowledges that their employees only live one life, in one time, as one person, the same as they do, they should immediately throw the performance review out of the window. Performance reviews are meaningless. Once we acknowledge that it is, first and foremost and above all else a human being who is sitting in front of us, it is absurd to believe that we can appraise just the part of the person who is the employee, separate from the rest of their being. It is impossible to isolate the 33% of the human mind that spends time at work from the remaining 67%, let alone have a meaningful conversation with it.

It comes as no great surprise that, according to a YouGov. org poll of the UK workforce,[57] more than half of all professionals describe appraisals as 'pointless' or 'time-consuming'. According to Gallup's research on the American workplace,[58] many managers struggle to conduct effective performance reviews with their employees. The report finds that the current version of performance reviews fails to provide clarity or a sense of meaning. In fact, only 23% of all employees think that their managers provide meaningful feedback. On the other hand, employees who claim to have had meaningful conversations with a manager about their goals and accomplishments are 2.8 times more likely to feel a sense of commitment to their jobs.

In principle, there is nothing wrong with the idea of a manager and employee meeting alone in a room and having a confidential conversation. In practice, however, it is a different matter. First, it often takes many attempts to fight our way past the hordes of middle management and assistants before we reach the management oracle. When we get there, we discover that what we thought would be an hour-long conversation about something heartfelt is more often than not a quick and superficial chat that leaves us with more professional questions than existential answers. The reason for this is that these conversations neither start from an existential position – the fundamental aspects of being – nor end with an existential perspective on the realization of our potential.

If we are to manage in a meaningful manner, what we need is a conversation based on the idea that work should be existential and intimate. The time we spend at work comes from the same pool as the time that we spend on any other activity. This conversation must not be a career-oriented one, aimed at evaluating the professional development needed to reach the next pay grade. It must be two individuals who care about and respect each other. The starting point is love, not exploitation. They both need to feel quite sincerely that pursuing the organization's purpose is meaningful.

The conversation must seek to identify what the employee would consider a meaningful life, as well as the barriers, in life and in work, that are preventing them from realizing it. This type of conversation presents a fundamental challenge to the concept of professional distance and the idea that time can be split. Every member of staff must be given the opportunity to present their whole life to their manager. They must also feel secure in the knowledge that the manager is effectively assuming co-responsibility for their whole life and, therefore, their wellbeing.

Saying "I love you" can be a huge and daunting step, both for the person saying it and the person hearing it. However, there are many ways to translate this form of platonic love into what we might call everyday or working language: "I like you," "I admire you" or "I place the utmost value on you." Irrespective of how you choose to say it, the moral is the same – to provide good management, you must love the people you manage. You must care for them. If they suffer, you suffer too.

It doesn't need to be an abstract concept, either. Take, for example, an employee (X) whose boyfriend lives in a different country. In her case, the conversation must address this problem. She must feel comfortable enough to say that he is finding their long-distance relationship difficult. She wants the best for him but also wants to give their relationship the best possible chance. Her manager must be able to trust her enough to organize and design the work in such a way that she can spend more time with her boyfriend while delivering the results expected of her.

What about her colleagues in production? They too can be led on the basis of platonic love. How? The manager explains their colleague's personal situation and tries to work with them to find a solution that everyone is happy with. Can we adjust the work schedules to ensure that X works just as many hours and is just as productive, but has every Friday and Monday off to visit her boyfriend? In a workplace with high MQ – or at least an ambition to achieve it – this should be possible. If not, then X's future in the company will be short-lived, as the degree of meaning in her life will be so low that she will have to choose between her job or her relationship, which is not a desirable outcome for her or the organization.

In the end, life is inherently unpredictable. Meaning is not found in the vagaries of fortune or misfortune, but in how we handle them. And that goes for both employees and managers.

6

HUMANISTIC
CAPITALISM

There is nothing inherently wrong with the quantum leap our civilization has taken in the last century. Indeed, the pace with which we have expanded the economy and improved opportunities has been truly impressive. The challenge is that these improvements appear to have been at the expense of existential progress and have not, therefore, led to people living better and more meaningful lives. However, we can't blame capitalism for that, as it is ultimately just a system for accumulating wealth, something at which it is damn good. It makes no promises about the content or nature of that prosperity and shouldn't be held accountable for any of its ramifications. It's up to us, as users of the system, to determine how we want to exploit the opportunities it offers. Given the increase in the number of people who are too anxious, stressed, depressed, lonely or medicated to find their way and meaning in life, the current trend has little to commend it. If we don't make a serious attempt to avoid the onrushing existential meltdown, we cannot be true to ourselves and look each other in the eye. However, this requires that we begin to ask ourselves what kind of wealth we want and then take a stand with regard to how it should be accumulated.

It's not a matter of opposing capitalism or shaming those who participate in it. For good or ill, it is difficult to identify any other system that has been as historically effective as capitalism in achieving its goals. One aspect of this is that capitalism has an unrivalled ability to elevate people out of poverty and illiteracy, at a pace that leaves all other -isms behind. There is every reason to believe that it is also capable of making an essential contribution to enhancing the quality and meaning of life. Our focus, therefore, ought to be on creating a new form of capitalism to ensure that social, economic and technological progress is *synchronous* with existential progress. However, this requires that we intervene and transform capitalism as we know it, without destroying or waging war on it.

First, it isn't just necessary, but also quite natural for capitalism to change its spots. In the 16th century, feudalism's barter economy, which had previously gained ground as an economic and military necessity due to a shortage of precious metals, gave way to monetary economics. Land and property became viable currencies, and the growth of state power led to the new states issuing their own notes and coins.

Around the mid 18th century, the first Industrial Revolution again began to transform capitalism. In most countries, the state financed and drove the Industrial Revolution. This led to the emergence of many of the monopolies that we have started to break up in recent decades to encourage a more free and competitive market economy.

Change, due to either military, economic, political or social necessity, is an integral part of capitalism's historical trajectory. The forces that, both now and in the immediate future, will put pressure on modern capitalism to change again are primarily existential in nature. Our existential health is under such pressure that it is starting to threaten the market economy. It is becoming more and more difficult to keep the promise of endlessly accumulating wealth. The people responsible for keeping the treadmill turning are running out of breath. No matter how much we raise our standard of living, there will never be any guarantee that it will automatically translate into a promise of mental wellbeing and a strong sense of meaningfulness. We may produce a financial and social surplus, but the meaningfulness of life is not defined by whether we register a surplus or a deficit in those columns. It is the way in which we deal with chance and life's many ups and downs that determines whether or not it fills us with meaning. Similarly, capitalism can never be meaningful *per se*. It's just a system. Whether or not a system is meaningful depends on how it is used.

This is why we need *humanistic capitalism*. Yes, we should chase profit and wealth, but the focus must always be on human beings, and it should never be at their expense. The lesson of humanistic capitalism is, therefore, that *the value of money depends on how it is earned*. It is no longer good enough that money is earned within the limits prescribed by the law. The traditional and dominant understanding of capitalism today is that as long as you earn your money legally, you can watch the bottom line improve with a clear conscience. We can no longer continue to delude ourselves and each other that this is the case. If every pound and dollar you earn incurs a cost in terms of increasing levels of stress, anxiety, loneliness and depression, both in the workplace and in society as a whole, then those pounds and dollars are worth less than ones that help to reduce these social and physical ills or perhaps even contribute to the general sense of meaningfulness. We need a form of capitalism in which the market regulates the value of money based on the moral demand that we put people before capital.

The basic principle of humanistic capitalism is that there is a difference between legality and morality. That something is legal doesn't necessarily mean it's also right in the moral sense. Legality is about evaluating whether something falls within legally defined standards. Morality, by contrast, is about whether something is virtuous – i.e., within the frameworks of what is considered decent, regardless of what the law may dictate. In the late medieval period, morality plays emerged as a way of teaching audiences about human virtues and vices, to show them the forces that vie for control of the human soul.

We might think that there would be no need for a medieval-style morality play to demonstrate that child labour isn't the most morally acceptable mode of production. Nevertheless, it wasn't until the mid-19th century that countries like Great Britain started to regulate it. And it was even later, with the Factory Act of 1878 and the Education Act of 1880, that legislation was enacted to eradicate the problem. Nevertheless, it was not prohibited until 1913. Until then, child labour was legal, but very few would argue that it was moral. Ironically, however, it was not morality that put an end to the widespread practice of child labour. It was primarily industrial progress. Other modes of production became so efficient that child labour became less economically viable. In other words, legality does not constitute sufficient grounds on which to assess whether something is right or wrong and definitely cannot be what regulates the value of money.

What we need is a transition to *humanistic* capitalism – a capitalism that, in its goals, means and justification, seeks to create meaning in people's lives. This is a form of capitalism that places demands not just on *what* we produce, but also *how* and *why* we produce it. It is a capitalism that makes a radical demand: that any added value, and any transaction, process or value chain associated with the production, must be able to pass the meaningfulness litmus test. The word order is crucial here. We do not need *capitalistic* humanism, as that would mean a commercialization of humanity, rather than a humanization of the commercial.

For instance, just think of how something as beautiful and thoroughly human as St Valentine's Day has, in modern times, become hyper-commercialized. What was intended to be a day to celebrate love, in honour of St Valentine, has become a ruthless profit machine – little more than a Black Friday with hearts and flowers. According to legend, in the third century, St Valentine was officiating Christian weddings in defiance of Emperor Claudius' orders. He was later arrested and beheaded. These days, his story rarely serves as a reminder that love takes precedence over legality, but it is a very good earner for florists and jewellers. The capitalist aspect is at the core, not the human side. It is no longer enough for capitalism to justify its positive effect on society by arguing that it has created jobs and growth. It must also have an existential and moral dimension if it is to serve us in the future.

But is it too idealistic to demand that companies and organizations strive to do more than just meet the minimum requirements of legality? Even if you're not convinced by the philosophical argument that modern capitalism does not create life with quality and meaning, consider the not insignificant commercial argument. It may be theoretically interesting to criticize economic prosperity for its lack of existential return, but what is the financial return on existential progress? In other words, if we demand that it should be possible to measure the value of money in terms of meaningfulness, what then is the monetary value of meaningfulness?

A study of the top 500 companies in the US[59] showed how those that are organized around a higher moral purpose and seek to make a difference in society perform better than more traditional companies. Over 15 years, so-called purpose-driven companies provided a return to their shareholders that was 14 times higher than the average business, and they also outperformed the average business in the short and medium term. This is not just didactic medieval dramaturgy – it is hard-nosed capitalist reasoning.

Each year, the Havas Group analyses what they define as meaningful brands.[60] The results clearly show that the majority of brands across markets are negatively affected by a lack of trust from consumers. Approximately 75% of consumers expect brands to contribute positively to the individual and collective quality of life. However, only 40% feel that this actually happens. In fact, we wouldn't give a damn if as many as 77% of the brands whose products we use every day disappeared from the face of the Earth, a 3%-point increase from the year before. The analysis shows, equally clearly, that brands perceived as meaningful by consumers ultimately outperform those that are not. Between 2006 and 2016, shareholders in companies with meaningful brands received a return that was 206% higher than the stock market average.

The claim that ethics and efficiency are somehow mutually exclusive is demonstrably absurd. The commercial is by no means incompatible with the existential. It has long been said that to maximize efficiency, productivity and performance, you must be tough. However, it is vital to base our actions on knowledge, rather than rhetoric and conjecture. Whether in politics, education or leadership development, if we use language that separates the 'hard' from the 'soft', we limit our potential. As far as society at large is concerned, this arbitrary division says nothing about actual differences in quality or utility. Why should numbers take precedence over letters? Why should the effect of a slap be greater than the effect of a kiss? It isn't, because ethics and efficiency are inextricably interwoven. The commercial and existential coexist and will continue to do so. It's as simple as that.

Consumer demand for meaningfulness is reflected in employees who demand precisely the same in their workplace and in the content and purpose of their work. A major study by McKinsey[61] shows that employees who consider their work meaningful are up to five times as productive as those for whom work is merely satisfactory. Similarly, studies show that employees who perceive their work as meaningful are 30% more innovative, 90% more engaged and 40% more loyal (in terms of retention) than employees who do not consider their work meaningful.[62] Further, from all the MQ analyses Voluntas have conducted since 2016 we have found that employees with a higher than average meaningfulness score report 24% lower levels of unbearable stress and significantly fewer sick days.[63] The more meaningfulness in our work, the higher the productivity and profitability and – with relevance for the 'idealistic'– the higher the quality of life.

The value of money is not its purchasing power or investment power. The value of money *is* the meaningfulness attached to it. The value of money must be measured against the meaningfulness created in the process of earning it, whether as a company, an investor, a manager or employee.

The value of money depends on how it is earned.

7

LOYALTY AND
MUTINY

In a scene from the movie *Pirates of the Caribbean: At World's End*, Elizabeth Swann and the rest of her crew are taken prisoner on the ghost ship *The Flying Dutchman*. The monstrous crew is made up of lost sailors who, in trade for dying at sea, have chosen to serve 100 years before the mast, under the command of Captain Davy Jones. What they probably weren't told when they signed the contract to escape death was that they would undergo a gradual and painful mutation from humans to marine monsters, before ending their days as part of the ship itself. For each year that passes, the crew becomes less and less human as their bodies take on the properties of creatures from the deep, until they eventually become one with the hull. "Part of the crew, part of the ship," goes their pirate motto.

During her captivity, Elizabeth Swann finds the mad sailor Bootstrap Bill, whose human form is all but obscured by algae and barnacles as, bit by bit, he is being assimilated into the ship. Elizabeth tells him that his son, William, has set out to save his father from this torment before the hull painfully consumes him, body and soul. However, Elizabeth finds to her horror that she may be too late. It appears that Bootstrap Bill's soul has already been consumed after many years in the service of Davy Jones. He and the ship are now one.

The fate of Bootstrap Bill and his fellow lost seafarers is a mischievous example of where misguided loyalty, albeit in this case semi-involuntary, can lead. If an employee asks no questions about the course plotted or the direction of travel, says nothing when they are going the wrong way, then they too risk becoming part of the ship, i.e., becoming institutionalised.

As a working person, where should your loyalty lie? First and foremost, with yourself and your meaning in life – and those closest to your heart. Next, with the organization's purpose and the virtues associated with it which connect your own individual sense of meaning to the organization's day-to-day work. The purpose is the compass by which you navigate. It sets the coordinates. It is vital that the organization's purpose is aligned with your own and brings meaning to the one life that you have. According to Gallup, employees who are able to link their goals to the organization's goals are 3.5 more likely to be engaged.[64]

Employees should not be appointed to be loyal to a boss or job title, but first and foremost to a purpose. If a manager acts in a way that is incompatible with the purpose and the organization's virtues, there is a moral obligation to respond accordingly and make the necessary change. At this point, you have two possible courses of action: jump ship, because you can no longer look at yourself in the mirror, or you commit mutiny and make the captain walk the plank. As the American professor of philosophy Robert C. Solomon aptly put it in 1992 then:

> While business life has its specific goals and distinctive practices and people in business have their particular concerns, loyalties, roles and responsibilities, there is no 'business world' apart from the people who work in business and the integrity of those people determines the integrity of the organization as well as vice versa.[65]

Organizations and corporations are human constructions and as such their morality relies on the virtuousness and integrity of the humans who embody them.

If an organization has managed to bring together a group of employees who share a similar outlook on life and who work for it because they want it to achieve its purpose, then they will never jeopardise their own or the organization's moral compass in trade for any short-term material gain. Because they are aware that the ethical and existentialistic risk outweighs the monetary reward.

THE DIFFERENCE BETWEEN VALUES AND VIRTUES

An organization's purpose is underpinned by a hierarchy of virtues that help achieve it. Virtues are the basic principles by which moral beings navigate. They are our deeply ingrained, often unconscious ideas about good and evil, right and wrong.

Virtues are arranged into a hierarchy so that we can distinguish between right and wrong, set our priorities and act accordingly. At the top of the hierarchy is the purpose, that which provides the most meaning, both for the individual and for the collective.

It is crucial to understand the essential difference between values and virtues. Many organizations claim to be value-based, but this often means little more than the values being listed in a strategic document, pasted on the wall in the reception or emblazoned on a website. However, neither people nor organizations (which are made up of people) can assign themselves a value. For example, being honest requires more than just saying, "We are honest." It is up to others to assess the extent to which that claim is true. If you must refer to your own values, then you must start with what others say about you.

A banal yet subtle example of this arose when a new hair salon displayed a neatly painted cardboard sign in their window to attract customers: "Trendy hair salon opening soon." However, trendiness is for others to decide; we can't assign ourselves an attribute or value. Rather, it is something we must prove through our words and actions – in this case, through every single haircut.

By comparison, virtues are not based on what others think we are, but instead on what we want to be, for example, "I want to be honest." If we take our starting point in what we are striving to be, we are also communicating that we are fallible. We are not perfect. By doing so, we underline that there is something we aspire to be, but which we have not yet fully achieved. While values are static states, virtues are something we aspire to be. They are instruments that develop the human characteristics of an individual and an organization. What we are really saying is, "I'm not always honest, but I constantly strive to be."

Virtues are linked to something existential. By giving our organization a philosophical, ethical and existential demand, we make it easier to start working on the basis of virtues rather than values.

The terms *value* and *virtue* stem from two different traditions. Economists talk about value as the result of a valuation. An item has utility value, a measure of the usefulness that makes it saleable. It also has an exchange value, i.e., a measure of its value relative to other goods. Virtue, however, emerged from moral philosophy and has quite different connotations. This brings us back to the concept of humanistic capitalism and its basic premise – that there is a difference between legality and morality. Just because something is legal does not necessarily mean it is moral. Morally, the value of money, goods, results and success is determined by how they were earned, created and achieved. Companies and organizations should set the bar higher than just legality by selecting and precisely defining the virtues that will inform their ethics and ultimately bring them closer to realizing their purpose. Human beings are essentially imperfect. For example, nobody is honest all the time, but it is a virtue to strive for, both individually and collectively, every single day. A virtue that is not followed up by action has no value and is as immoral as a financial report containing false figures. Enron, the energy company who in 2001 became a reference point in the history of corporate scandals, had a core value of "Integrity". Similarly, Volkswagen, the German car manufacturer which rigged millions of vehicles to cheat diesel emissions, stated in its values that "We act with integrity". To judge from the systemic 'Teflonic Identity Manoeuvring' shown by individuals inside the strategic apex of both organizations, these value statements were not translated into virtues that invariably served as a moral code of conduct preached and enforced every single day. They remained wallpaper.

SELF-AWARENESS AS A MEANS TO UNDERSTANDING YOUR PURPOSE AND VIRTUES

The Swiss psychiatrist and founder of analytical psychology Carl Gustav Jung left an intellectual legacy that has inspired both artists and researchers. Jung had a close working relationship with Sigmund Freud. Jung was the younger of the two, but they nonetheless had a profound influence on each other. Like Freud, Jung worked with many different aspects and layers of the human psyche. They had a particular shared interest in the study of the subconscious and how our inner values are expressed in dreams and fantasies. As human beings, our actions are determined by hierarchies of principles, virtues and ideas. The very existence of these hierarchies is extremely important – not all virtues are equally worthy or valued equally by everybody. Quite simply, it is impossible to do anything unless you believe that one option is better than another. Otherwise, why would you act at all? Right now, you are reading this book; therefore, you thought that reading this book was preferable to not reading it or to doing something else. This is an example, albeit a small one, of a hierarchy of virtues at work.

All of us act, consciously or subconsciously, on the basis of a built-in hierarchy of virtues. The actions you perform and the virtues you live by therefore say more about you than what you think about yourself. What you believe is true, good or right is expressed more clearly in the consequences of your actions than in your purported beliefs. Unfortunately, it is highly unlikely that we fully comprehend these hierarchies of virtues. Humans are the most complex creatures on Earth, but if we can't even figure out how to adjust the clock on the oven to daylight savings time, how can we expect to understand what we consist of fully? Subconsciously or not, if we are treated in a way that is not in alignment with our virtues or our ethics, we turn to anger or despair. When this happens, our hierarchy of virtues comes to the fore and shows its colours.

Not only are our virtues sometimes subconscious, but they are also arranged into several fragmented and possibly conflicting hierarchies. As such, you may find some decisions impossibly difficult, or you might have mixed emotions about something you do.

Once again, we find ourselves back at the Temple of Apollo at Delphi: 'Know thyself'. It takes a great deal of self-aware-ness, both as an organization and as a human being, to be able to understand our hierarchy of virtues. Only once we have done so can we answer the most fundamental question: "What is the meaning of life?" The relationship between purpose and virtues is both fundamental and intimate. Hierarchies of virtues – be it our own or an organization's – do not exist in and of themselves but are created in response to a demand or some other factor. One such factor is the overarching purpose. Our virtues act as magnetic fields that point in the same direction; toward our highest purpose.

However, as mentioned, virtues are dynamic and changeable. We can aspire to a virtue without it being dominant in our behaviour. Indeed, we have the opportunity to take control of our virtues by making the subconscious conscious, by increasing our self-awareness and redefining the virtues that we want to determine our lives. It might be said that we all have virtues that point toward a higher purpose, but that they are subject to constant change and refinement. Virtues are what we want to be. They are what we strive for.

Part of this striving entails asking others to give us feedback, honestly and authoritatively, and to remind us of who we want to be, in order to ensure that we live in accordance with our virtues. Just as an external auditor is needed to approve a company's accounts, we should, as part of our own internal bookkeeping, allow ourselves to be evaluated and thus ensure that we live our lives in a way that is consistent with what we want.

In this way, virtues are properties or principles that we, either alone or with others, have consciously defined as the characteristics to which we must adhere in order to live our lives with self-respect and meaning.

MUTINY – HOW FAR SHOULD YOU GO AS AN INDIVIDUAL?

As individuals, how far should we go to maintain our self-respect? If we ask no questions, and if we fail to maintain self-respect, we will end up like the doomed seamen on *The Flying Dutchman*. Unless we want to end up with a beard full of mussels, metaphorically speaking of course, and slowly become indistinguishable from our workplace, which may be heading in a different direction from the one we have plotted for ourselves, then there are only two responsible ways of taking your fate into your own hands: jump overboard or mutiny. It's as simple as that. It is essential that there is an overlap between our own virtues and purpose and those of the organization.

The time we spend working is taken from somewhere else – it is time that could be spent with our children, our family, our closest friends or on our own. In a way, it is the ultimate zero-sum game. For the philosopher or artist, the fusion is obvious. Even when down the pub and without a pen or brush, the philosopher and artist are still at work, because the creative process never stops. For inscrutable reasons, we have tacitly decided that this does not apply to other working people. We have decided that we should not demand that work offer much in the way of existential meaning. We must find that elsewhere, usually in a place where we spend less time than we do at work.

We commonly hear phrases like, "It's not about you, it's about what's best for the company." As well as being one of the most off-putting sentences ever uttered, it's also a pretty illogical thing to say. What we are being asked to do is to reduce our lives – the one life that we have – to something subordinate to a commercial identity, to something of lesser value than a company registration number.

Our work must have an existential starting point. If we have acknowledged that the existential direction of our one life does not overlap with what the organization has to offer, or if the organization is straying from an otherwise well-defined and meaningful course, we must resist. Indeed, once we have discovered that our work is meaningless, we have a responsibility, not just to ourselves but also to the organization, to act. We must mobilize the integrity, courage and self-respect to stand in constructive opposition. Through diligence and perseverance, we must seek to change the organization's direction. In other words, we must stage a mutiny and, metaphorically speaking, throw the captain overboard, right the ship and ensure that whatever we are all working toward gives the best possible meaning, not only for the organization, but also, first and foremost, for us.

If we don't want to do that, the only other option is to leave. If we lack the will or courage to change course, or if the resistance is too great, we must jump ship. Hand in our notice. Pack our bags and go on our way. But we must do it loudly, so no one is in any doubt that we fought to the last to be allowed to realize the meaning of our lives. In doing so, we help others open their eyes, break out of pluralistic ignorance and free themselves from the ship's hull that threatens to consume them. It is also worth thinking about whether voicing a strong opinion on the way out of the door, for example at an exit interview, might help bring about change and improve the lot of former colleagues.

Another lesson we can take from Jung is a fine-tuning of the otherwise deeply ingrained 'golden rule', the moral principle that says that you should "treat others as you would wish to be treated." Namely, that it is not an admonition, but rather a virtue, the goal of which is balance. No matter whether we are interacting with our boss, colleagues, friends or life partners, we are duty-bound to state our case clearly, just as they are to state theirs. We are just as duty-bound as they are to carry ourselves with the same self-respect and adhere just as strongly to our virtues. It's about standing tall, rejecting self-contempt and carrying ourselves with the necessary self-respect to mount constructive opposition when others seek to override our (and the organization's) moral compass. The earlier in life we choose not to accept any form of repression, the greater the probability that we will live a dignified life. Dignity is central to a sense of meaning.

As working people, we have every reason not to be victims, not to be slaves. We are free, damn it! And if we end up in a situation where we realize that the one life we have is not characterized by self-respect and driven by the search for the greatest possible meaning, we must have the self-respect to opt out and move on. Sometimes, the sweetest poetry that can flow from our lips is the phrase "I quit."

Nowadays, more and more people are quitting their jobs due to an urge to escape, rather than in pursuit of something different. In most cases, this involves *opting out* of the status quo rather than *opting into* something else. In other words, when employees abandon ship, it is often because they have not tried, or at least not succeeded in, changing their existing situation.

HOW FAR SHOULD AN ORGANIZATION GO TO DEFEND ITS PURPOSE?

If we, as individuals and employees, want to try to bring about the change needed to maximize meaning, must we do everything in our power – even staging a mutiny, if necessary – to defend the organization's purpose? The short answer is "yes." The long answer is "hell, yes!"

If the organization really is purpose-driven, then decisions about recruitment, promotion, demotion and dismissal ought to be based on whether the individual applying for a job, looking for promotion or staying in the company is driven by the same purpose as the organization. Before assessing their technical and professional skills, you should consider whether they truly believe in the company's purpose, and are therefore able to live by and implement it. The next step is to determine whether they possess the requisite technical and formal skills.

Usually, that is not what happens. In most cases, people only look at the applicant's technical competencies, the specialist knowledge that the organization needs. If they have them, they're in. The same thoroughness is rarely brought to bear on whether the candidate's humanity, mentality, idealism and ideology resonate with the organization's purpose.

We usually hire people because of their technical and professional potential, not their human potential to achieve the company's purpose. Not only does this dilute the purpose and make it superfluous, but it is also inefficient and unintelligent. If you want the recruitment process to be a success, based on whether the successful applicant performs to the best of their abilities, the individual concerned must thrive in the job.

As we have established, wellbeing is inextricably linked to the meaning in our jobs. The individual concerned must be able to see a more profound and higher purpose. Hiring someone who doesn't believe in the organization's work, direction and overall purpose is simply absurd. Imagine, for example, an atheist trying to become a member of a religious community. It just doesn't make sense! So, if an organization wants to create something sustainable, then its purpose must also serve as its primary organizing principle. The best strategy is to hire and retain employees who believe in its purpose.

Returning to the ship metaphor, we might somewhat cynically reformulate it as follows: we need to dump some of the dead weight overboard. In other words, we must let go of those who are in passive opposition to the organization's actual course and therefore in passive opposition to their own lives. Those who don't inject or receive energy or inspire change, but rather suck others into their whirlpool of negativity. Quite simply, they don't find meaning in what they are doing, which leaves them frustrated and despondent. The most humane way to optimize an organization is to remove those who don't find meaning within it and help them to realize their human potential elsewhere.

Managers should be guided, at all times, by two things. First, we should ask ourselves whether our leadership is humane and inspirational and has contributed to the realization of the human potential around us. This can only happen if the individual concerned has a high level of meaning in their life as a result of their work. Second, we ought, in particular, to relate to those who still don't find the meaning they seek even when management is humane and inspirational. For their sake, and for that of the organization, we should help them find that meaning somewhere else. That way, they won't end up being resentful wage slaves, but will instead be mobilized to realize their human potential. Additionally, managers ought to undergo their own regular evaluations to understand the extent to which they have lived up to the organization's purpose.

The task of a manager is to be the 'chief meaningfulness officer' – the one who has responsibility for and takes the lead in maintaining and expressing the meaningfulness of the organization's purpose. To stop this just being a naïve appeal to their good will, managers must also be held accountable for their leadership and the mechanisms for this oversight must lie with a board or some other strategic management body, not with the managers themselves.

Like all human beings, we are fallible; we could be wrong. We may think that our leadership is humane and inspirational, or that we have already created frameworks for meaning in the workplace. We may think that we act, every day, in ways that help fulfil the organization's purpose. But what if we are about to lose a member of staff who we feel is a dead weight, but the individual concerned is actually on the right track? Perhaps they can't quite summon the courage to make a stand, or they may even have fallen victim to intimidation from management or others.

The organization should provide the necessary frameworks to make room for 'rebellion' and adapt to challenges before there are mutinies. This may sound extreme, but it is already becoming accepted, and even embedded in their structures, by some of the world's biggest companies. They call it 'corporate activism'. For example, in Coca-Cola's headquarters in Atlanta, a whole department has been tasked with systematizing and incorporating the activism of more than 700,000 employees. The reason they are doing this is that some of the world's biggest brands have recognized that in order to attract and retain good staff, it is no longer enough just to roll up and spout patronizing rhetoric about how nothing is bigger than the organization itself. In short, they are making room for activism in order to avoid mutiny.

This is the first level of the management principles that underpin meaningfulness; namely, that the day-to-day executive management of an organization should be measured, reviewed and held accountable on the basis of its ability to create meaning for the members of the organization.

ALL OF US ACT, CONSCIOUSLY OR SUBCONSCIOUSLY, ON THE BASIS OF A BUILT-IN HIERARCHY OF VIRTUES. THE ACTIONS YOU PERFORM AND THE VIRTUES YOU LIVE BY THEREFORE SAY MORE ABOUT YOU THAN WHAT YOU THINK ABOUT YOURSELF. WHAT YOU BELIEVE IS TRUE, GOOD OR RIGHT IS EXPRESSED MORE CLEARLY IN THE CONSEQUENCES OF YOUR ACTIONS THAN IN YOUR PURPORTED BELIEFS. UNFORTUNATELY, IT IS HIGHLY UNLIKELY THAT WE FULLY COMPREHEND THESE HIERARCHIES OF VIRTUES. HUMANS ARE THE MOST COMPLEX CREATURES ON EARTH, BUT IF WE CAN'T EVEN FIGURE OUT HOW TO ADJUST THE CLOCK ON THE OVEN TO DAYLIGHT SAVINGS TIME, HOW CAN WE EXPECT TO UNDERSTAND WHAT WE CONSIST OF FULLY?

8

HOW FAR SHOULD
WE GO AS A SOCIETY?

One December day in 1997, in the former Japanese capital of Kyoto, several world leaders met to sign an agreement aimed at protecting the Earth's climate. The agreement was designed to ensure that by 2012, industrialized countries would reduce their greenhouse gas emissions by 5% compared with the level in 1990. The treaty was intended to achieve "stabilization of greenhouse gas concentrations in the atmosphere at a level that would prevent dangerous anthropogenic interference with the climate system."[66]

Why was it necessary to bring together the world's leaders and enter into an agreement? How had we reached the point where the next step was a formal pact? Why did we need to set hard targets and regulate the global market economy?

Researchers first predicted the greenhouse effect and rising global temperatures back in the late 19th century, but their theories did not reach a wider scientific audience until the mid-1960s. Eventually, it was widely recognized that climate change posed a real threat and that the villain of the piece was the emission of greenhouse gases.

The challenges of climate change and global warming had become so large that they could no longer be overlooked. How do we respond in a situation like that? Either the market and ordinary people react in unison – with individuals and organizations using their own free will and freedom to address the challenges – or we turn to political regulation. In the three decades after a majority of scientists broadly had agreed that the way we treated the climate was untenable, the market and the people, left to their own devices, had done almost nothing. That is why political action was needed.

It took more than 30 years for the Kyoto Protocol to be drawn up. It then took a further eight years to ratify the agreement. Since then, there has been an alarming reluctance to introduce market-driven climate adaptations and new climate agreements and for the world's largest economies to arrive at a consensus. We may now have reached the point of no return. It is even debatable whether we can still curb temperature rises before it is too late.

This brings us back to the core of humanistic capitalism. The climate debate shows that the value of money depends on how it is earned. Although most organizations' Corporate Social Responsibility (CSR) initiatives leave such enormous scope for interpretation that they can act like a black hole, there is no doubt that money earned with minimal climate and environmental impact has a higher value. Most of us do care and would prefer that everybody takes care of the planet while earning their money.

However, if it is obvious that climate impact should be monitored and subject to quotas and reporting, is it impossible to imagine doing the same for stress, depression and anxiety? If we are capable of regulating the air that surrounds us, is it so unrealistic to imagine regulating the meaning that work contributes to our lives?

We are now in a situation that, in several ways, is reminiscent of the climate debate in the late 20th century. The workforce is increasingly lonely, depressed and stressed, and the problem has grown so big that it can no longer be overlooked or ignored. If business owners, organizations and the market fail to make changes, regulation is inevitable.

Imagine a reality in which it is a legal requirement for companies, in their yearly planning, to indicate how many people they expect will be made sick while generating shareholder value and salaries and bonuses for senior executives. Why is that an unreasonable demand? Why is it not the most natural thing in the world? Who, in all good conscience, would argue that this is not valuable knowledge, both for the company's owners and for the public? We have already reviewed the economic benefits of employees feeling a high degree of meaning, so other than the fact that it is the right thing to do, it is also something upon which shareholders should insist.

You might ask why capitalism should accept this responsibility when its purpose is to make money. The answer is quite clear – because not doing so is both immoral and unprofitable. First, it is immoral to exploit human potential in the pursuit of profit. Second, it is inefficient that our pursuit of short-term profit leads to an increasing proportion of the workforce being stressed, lonely, depressed and anxious. In other words, our current approach to both business and society is inefficient and unsustainable from the perspective of both the company and society as a whole.

Child labour didn't stop because we ran out of child workers, but because it was inefficient and immoral. We will hopefully soon come to the same collective realization about work-related ailments.

This brings us to the second level of the management principles that underpin meaningfulness. This consists of obliging organizations to document, based on a clearly defined methodology and precisely operationalized parameters, the extent to which they create meaning for their employees. It also entails holding them financially accountable for the costs – to employees, shareholders and society – associated with wellbeing languishing at socially unacceptable levels.

FROM GDP TO HAPPINESS INDEX
TO MEANINGFULNESS INDEX

For the last century or so, Gross Domestic Product (GDP) – commonly calculated as the sum total of a nation's goods and services, minus the resources used – has been the primary measure of growth. However, it has been criticized since the 1970s, and an increasing number of economists now believe that it is not a true and fair indicator of growth and economic progress. Nevertheless, it is still considered one of the most important economic indicators when commenting on the state of national economies. GDP is even frequently interpreted as an indicator of wellbeing, even though it is solely a measure of economic activity.

Factors such as nature and the environment are not taken into account in the calculations. Quite simply, they fall outside of the measurement system, as does everything else that is unrelated to production. Even the father of GDP, the Russian-American economist and Nobel Laureate Simon Kuznets, warned that it was not a suitable measure of society's wellbeing.[67]

It is, therefore, a huge paradox that, almost since the indicator's inception, we have not only let it drive the political agenda, but we have almost worshipped it, even though it says nothing about the difference between the goods produced. It doesn't distinguish between the value of basic goods and luxury goods, between goods that are destroying the environment and those that protect it. Nor is there any distinction between whether something improves or detracts from human wellbeing and social development.

Consensus is growing that GDP as an indicator does not tell the whole story. A number of alternatives have been proposed in recent decades. The UN launched what it calls the 'Human Development Index', which measures life expectancy, education and gross national income compared with per capita purchasing power. The World Economic Forum recently developed the 'Inclusive Development Index', which among other things addresses poverty, CO_2 footprints and inequality. The World Bank, too, has been experimenting with new ways of measuring prosperity.

In other words, not only is there a growing consensus among economists that GDP should be supplemented with other yardsticks by which to measure growth and prosperity, but the many indices are also increasingly acknowledging that other and better indicators should be used to provide a better basis on which to analyse our wellbeing and standard of living.

Nonetheless, the growth ideology remains generally accepted, and none of the alternative indices mentioned takes significant account of regression or progression in human life – i.e., existential conditions – and how better frameworks might improve our mental wellbeing. In fact, such parameters are only included when things have gone seriously wrong, when it is not only a case of meaninglessness and potential mental problems but actual clinical diagnoses such as depression and anxiety disorders. We measure ourselves – and manage ourselves – using the wrong parameters and using the indicators reactively. Only after the accounts have been drawn up do we find out how many people's health was sacrificed to boost GDP by 1.9%.

We use measurements of performance indicators and associated targets, which are known appositely as *lagging indicators*.

By measuring the result of a process, these indicators enable us to look back on it and evaluate whether we have done well enough. In other words, if there are problems, we don't know about them until afterward, by which time it is too late to do anything about it. It's a bit like an archaeological dig – we are always one step behind.

Instead, we need *leading indicators* that provide a clear picture of whether the existential foundation we are building is stable and will not crack. We need to determine in advance whether we are on the right path to achieve the results we seek.

Given that we need new and better indicators, is it so inconceivable that one of them should be the degree of meaning? Should meaningfulness not be a leading indicator of where we as a society should intervene? What if we stop measuring the degree of happiness and look at the level of meaning instead? What would it mean if we collectively sought a meaningful life rather than a happy one? Would this lead us, as individuals, to place a higher value on contexts that are not about being happy, but that seek to enhance self-awareness and lead us to a more meaningful life?

What would it mean for our social institutions and our businesses if they were judged on the degree of meaning they help generate? What would it mean if we measured education and training on the level of meaning they generate, rather than whether they are completed in the prescribed time? Would it change, for example, how nurses, teachers or police officers feel if the calling that led to their choice of job in the first place was clearly reflected in their day-to-day work? What if work was fundamentally meaningful?

Imagine a reality in which we do not struggle to climb the happiness ladder and achieve the highest rankings in a superficial happiness index, but instead strive for the greatest possible self-awareness and degree of meaning in life. Imagine a reality in which nations not only boasted about being the happiest on the planet but also the ones whose people experience the most *meaning*.

The third level of the management principles that underpin meaningfulness could, therefore, consist of every member of the United Nations committing to, based on precisely defined methodology and operationalised parameters, documenting how meaningful their citizens consider life to be.

EPILOGUE

This book was conceived on a July day about a decade ago, when I buried my father. His funeral taught me that even something deeply unhappy can still be one of the most meaningful events of our lives. In saying goodbye to him, I acknowledged him for the life he had lived and the uncompromising manner in which he had lived it. I thanked him for the lessons he had taught us and forgave him for the mistakes he made along the way. I looked at those he left behind, safe in the knowledge that we are all the richer for his presence. I observed his grandchildren and was filled with the conviction that faith in the future is not an empty and naïve hope.

If something as difficult as saying a final farewell to one of the people you admire and love the most can also be one of life's most meaningful experiences, then it seems a relatively modest aspiration to insist on seeking meaning in all other facets of life. We need to respect that when time has passed, it does not come back. Only in this way can we live a meaningful life. A life we can justify. A life we find acceptable. A life we can endorse because it enhances our sense of our own worth and dignity.

Most of us find it difficult to live this way. And yet we understand intuitively that when we arrive late for an appointment with another person, we are effectively robbing that person of their time. We have shortened the life they have left to live. In our haste, we must be careful that we don't start turning up late for our own lives. Every moment we spend working dutifully – day in and day out, year after year – at a job that, in both form and content, has absolutely no meaning for us, is gone forever. As such, we should not tolerate the fact that far too few managers understand that they are managing other people's time and therefore their lives. Managing them entails a particular obligation to get to know these people, to be interested in them, to understand their lives, empathize with their situation, contribute to their life's purpose, suffer with them, like them, even love them.

No matter how much we duck and dive, no matter how many coaches and conceptual gymnasts claim that it's all just a question of balance between work and leisure – or work and life – we can't begin to address the problem until we acknowledge that life just doesn't work that way. People aren't made that way. Time doesn't work that way. The semantics of the contradiction between work and life only serve to emphasize the absurdity of us imagining that one of the most serious problems of our age can be solved with catchphrases that only reinforce misguided notions about the basis for human existence.

We enjoy unprecedented levels of prosperity and technological progress, but we allow ourselves to make incomprehensibly small demands on our work and the managers who assign and organize it. As a result, our existential immune systems find it increasingly difficult to withstand the pressure and the uncertainty to which they are exposed. This is one of the main reasons for our poor mental health. My aim with this book is to declare war on the meaninglessness that plagues our lives. I want us all to develop enough existential equity to insist that we don't spend as much as a nanosecond on working, managing and making money in a way that would leave us waffling or dumbstruck when we are asked on our deathbed whether it was all worth it. If that requires giving up high salaries, grand titles, company cars or gilt-edged stock options, then so be it. A meaningful life takes precedence over everything.

I am very much aware that it can sound naïve to assert that meaningfulness comes before everything else – let alone that we can create organizations and companies based on this philosophy that not only deliver results but grow even faster and more efficiently. I also know that it may sound controversial to try to encourage intimacy between people who have been brought up to keep their distance from each other. But I would insist even more forcefully that what threatens the modern person's existential immune system is actually maintaining the arm's length principle that insists upon a clear divide between work and leisure, and which leads to an absence of intimacy during half of our waking hours.

To those who insist on the separation of work and leisure and consider abolishing it irresponsible, I would contend that precisely the opposite is true. What is irresponsible is vigorously defending a principle best illustrated by the concept of work-life balance. Since the late 1970s and early 1980s, this idea has been relentlessly pushed as the only way to help working people find joy in their life. And yet, during the same period, more and more people have been made sick by their work. In other words, more of the same will never be the solution.

We have drifted so far off course that the most recent arrivals to the labour market are the hardest hit. As part of Mental Health Awareness Week, the Mental Health Foundation in the UK carried out a stress survey on more than 4,500 people.[68] Interestingly, the findings were that millennials feel more under pressure at work than their baby boomer colleagues.

Twenty-eight per cent reported that stress was an expected part of their job. One third of millennials also said that stress makes them less productive at work. Futhermore, 61% of millennials suffer high or above-average stress, compared with 33% of the baby boomer generation and 50% of generation X.[69]

However, while looking at my own and my brothers' children at my father's funeral, I was filled with optimism and hope. I could see the outlines of the people they will one day become. I saw them starting to learn who they are and want to be, and who they are not and do not want to be. They want to be people with meaning and will.

Likewise, I am also filled with optimism by the fact that, in recent years, we have witnessed how young people, and especially the next generation, refuse to accept being reduced to a GPA but are demanding that the life they live and the work they do should be meaningful. I enjoy knowing and working with many young people who embody this spirit. One of them, Nic, was among the first employees that I hired four years ago. We became acquainted with each other at a job interview conducted via a poor Skype connection between Copenhagen and California. At first, there was no indication that this particular young man was anything more than the immaculate, well-groomed exterior that was apparent even through a badly pixelated screen. Nevertheless, it took him less than ten minutes to convince me that I had no choice but to hire him. When I asked why he thought that working with me would give his life value, he replied – as if it were the most natural thing in the world – that he wanted all major elements in his life to be driven by a purpose and an ethic that was worth fighting for. He said that his aim in life above all was to become as aware and clear as humanly possible about who he was and wanted to be and that through his work, he could realize that potential.

During my career, I have encountered many young people who tried to convince me to hire them. But the answer he gave me that day was the best I had ever heard. It's people like Nic whom I want to lead my children when they grow up and join the workforce. I find a sense of peace in that – not least because there is every reason to believe that in the future, many more will be cast from the same mould.

According to UN data,[70] 32% of the global population are young people from the self-aware Generation Z (born between the mid-1990s and the mid-2000s), which is a bigger group than the previous generation of millennials. My optimism is further boosted by the fact that these young people can look forward to the usual old management methodologies, business models and investment profiles being challenged and even replaced by new types of organizations and companies – ones that are not ashamed of making money and don't sacrifice their purpose to do so, companies whose business model *is* their purpose and the meaningfulness that justifies it, and whose management operates on that basis.

They're out there. I've met them. You've met them. And there are more and more of them every day. There is, therefore, every reason for optimism. We can look forward to a future in which more and more of us, when the end comes, will be able to reflect on our one life, lived in one time, by one person, and feel that we wasted as little of it as possible.

ACKNOWLEDGMENTS

In at least one way, writing a book is like assembling IKEA flat-pack furniture. Every time you face doing it again, you naively believe that it will be easy. And every time, it turns out to be exactly the opposite. When the idea of this book began to take shape, it was very clear in my head. The key messages. The concepts. The data. The argumentation. When I started to put everything into words and when people began responding positively, I thought, "This book is writing itself!" But it wasn't. Just as the previous three hadn't. There is a crucial difference between thinking, speaking and writing. For all three, the message is (hopefully) the same, but thought, speech and writing are different forms of expression and place different demands on the communicator.

I owe a large number of people a debt of gratitude for their various invaluable contributions to the project and for helping me to transform my thoughts and spoken words into a reasonably coherent book.

Above all, thanks to the philosopher Nicolai Ellemann Iversen ('Nic') for enriching my life with his strong faith, beautiful mind, deep intellect, great loyalty and impressive diligence. In recent years, he has been the best philosophical sounding board anyone could wish for. This book is just as much his as it is mine. Next, a big thank you to my editor, Mette Korsgaard, for her warmth and professionalism, and to LID Publishing for amplifying my philosophy. To professor in literature Lasse Horne Kjældgaard and professor in psychology

Lene Tanggaard for their invaluable input and guidance. And to my two dear friends Torsten Hvidt and Jakob Jensen for their critical eye and sharp attention to mistakes, errors and ambiguities.

Warm thanks are also due to Lasse Wagner for his hard work, thoroughness and perspicacity when he stepped in as the process came to a head. It is also important to thank all of the people who, by virtue of their curiosity and courage, had enough faith in me to make their lives, companies and organizations available to my philosophical laboratory. Of those, Kaspar Basse, in particular, stands out – with his vision, great courage and steely determination, he has put meaningfulness at the epicentre of one of the world's fastest-growing retail concepts and afforded me the privilege of being a participant in this process. Additionally, I also want to express my sincere gratitude to Sam and Holly Branson, Essie North and Noah Devereux for inviting me into the Big Change family and for all the inspiration it has given me.

Last, but by no means least, thank you to my wife, Sara, and our children, Emilia, Asger and Elliot, for being the zenith of my existence, the prism through which I see the world, and the catalyst for my meaningfulness – and for loving me, even though the time spent producing this book will not come again.

ENDNOTES

1   Ware, Bronnie. *The Top Five Regrets Of The Dying.*
    London: Hay House, 2012.
2   Jensen, Heidi Amalie Rosendahl, Michael Davidsen,
    Ola Ekholm, and Anne Illemann Christensen.
    Danskernes Sundhed – Den Nationale Sundhedsprofil 2017.
    Sundhedsstyrelsen, 2018.
3   Weforum.org. "The world has never been a better
    place. Don't believe us? Look at this chart." Last
    modified November 2016. https://www.weforum.org/
    agenda/2016/11/the-world-has-never-been-a-better-place.
4   Global Council for Happiness and Wellbeing.
    Global Happiness and Wellbeing – Policy report 2019.
    Global Council for Happiness and Wellbeing, 2019.
5   World Health Organization. *Depression and Other
    Common Mental Disorders: Global Health Estimates.*
    Licence: CC BY-NC-SA 3.0 IGO.
    Geneva: World Health Organization, 2017.
6   World Health Organization. *WHO Global Burden
    of Disease: 2004 Update.*
    Geneva: World Health Organization, 2008.
7   World Health Organization. *Depression and Other
    Common Mental Disorders: Global Health Estimates.* Licence:
    CC BY-NC-SA 3.0 IGO.
    Geneva: World Health Organization, 2017.
8   Khazan, Olga. "How loneliness begets loneliness."
    The Atlantic, April 6, 2017.

9   The Mary Foundation: "Ensomhed," 2019; Jensen,
    Heidi Amalie Rosendahl, Michael Davidsen, Ola Ekholm,
    and Anne Illemann Christensen. *Danskernes Sundhed –
    Den Nationale Sundhedsprofil 2017*. Sundhedsstyrelsen,
    2018.; Skovlund, Charlotte Wessel, Lars Vedel Kessing,
    Lina Steinrud Mørch & Øjvind Lidegaard: Increase in
    depression diagnoses and prescribed antidepressants
    among young girls. A national cohort study 2000–2013,
    Nordic Journal of Psychiatry, 2017.

10 Gallup. *State of the Global Workplace.*
    New York: Gallup Press, 2017.

11 Harter, Jim. "Dismal Employee Engagement Is a Sign of
    Global Management," *Gallup.com*, Dec 2017.

12 Mental Health Foundation. *Stress: Are we coping?*
    London: Mental Health Foundation, May 2018.

13 Dahlin, Eric, Erin Kelly, and Phyllis Moen. "Is work the new
    neighborhood? Social ties in the workplace, family, and
    neighborhood." *The Sociological Quarterly. 49. 719 – 736*, 2008.

14 Sørensen, Villy. *Uden Mål - Og Med: Moralske Tanker.*
    Copenhagen: Gyldendal, 1973.

15 St Augustine. *The Confessions*, n.d.

16 Alvesson, Mats, and Maxine Robertson. "Money Matters:
    Teflonic Identity Manoeuvring In The Investment
    Banking Sector." *Organization Studies 37* (1): 7-34, 2015.

17 National Occupational Mortality Surveillance (NOMS).
    US Department of Health and Human Services, Public
    Health Service, Centers for Disease Control and
    Prevention, National Institute for Occupational Safety
    and Health, Division of Surveillance, Hazard Evaluation
    and Field Studies, Surveillance Branch, 2015.

18 Gulati, Daniel. "The Top Five Career Regrets."
Harvard Business Review, December 2012.

19 Prince's Trust. "Youth Index 2019," 2019.
Due P, Diderichsen F, Meilstrup C, Nordentoft M, Obel
C, Sandbæk A. *Børn og unges mentale helbred. Forekomst af
psykiske symptomer og lidelser og mulige forebyggelsesindsatser.*
København: Vidensråd for Forebyggelse. 2014.

20 Dunn, Elizabeth W., and Michael Norton.
Happy Money: The science of smarter spending.
New York: Simon & Schuster, 2013.

21 Dunn, Elizabeth W., and Michael Norton.
Happy Money: The science of smarter spending.
New York: Simon & Schuster, 2013.

22 Lacan, Jacques. *My Teaching.* London: Verso Books, 2009.

23 Nietzsche, Friedrich. *On the Future of Our Educational
Institutions.* First Lecture, 1872.

24 Kevin Eagan, Ellen B. Stolzenberg, Joseph J. Ramirez,
Melissa C. Aragon, Maria R. Suchard, and Sylvia Hurtado.
The American freshman: National norms fall 2014.
Los Angeles: Higher Education Research Institute,
UCLA, 2014.

25 Kierkegaard, Søren. *Enten – Eller. Et Livs-Fragment.*
Copenhagen: Victor Eremita, 1843.

26 Brown, Jonathon D. "Understanding the better than
average effect: motives (still matter)." Personality and
Social Psychology Bulletin, 2012.

27 Sedikides, Constantine, Rosie Meek, Mark D. Alicke,
and Sarah Taylor. "Behind bars but above the bar: Prisoners
consider themselves more prosocial than non-prisoners."
British Journal of Social Psychology, 53, (2014): 396–403.

28 Blixen, Karen, "Kardinalens første Historie" (1957),
in Blixen, Karen. *Sidste Fortællinger*, Gyldendal, 2017.

29 Kruger, Justin, and David Dunning. "Unskilled and
Unaware of It: How Difficulties in Recognizing One's Own
Incompetence Lead to Inflated Self-Assessments." *Journal of
Personality and Social Psychology. 77* (6), (1999): 1121–1134.

30 World Health Organization. "Suicide Across The World," 2016.

31 Perlow, Leslie A., Constance Noonan Hadley,
and Eunice Eun. "Stop the Meeting Madness."
Harvard Business Review (*July-August 2017 issue*), 2017.

32 IDA. *Jobskifte og motivation for mobilitet.* IDA, 2016.

33 Waters, Sarah, Marina Karanikolos, and Martin McKee.
"When Work Kills." *Journal Of Public Mental Health 15* (4)
(2016): 229-234. doi:10.1108/jpmh-06-2016-0026.

34 Waters, Sarah, Marina Karanikolos, and Martin McKee.
"When Work Kills." *Journal Of Public Mental Health 15* (4)
(2016): 229-234. doi:10.1108/jpmh-06-2016-0026.

35 Bryson, Alex, and George Mackerron. "Are You Happy
While You Work?" *Economic Journal.* 127 (2016): 106-125.

36 Bryson, Alex, and George Mackerron. "Are You Happy
While You Work?" *Economic Journal.* 127 (2016): 106-125.

37 Zaleznik, Abraham. "Managers and leaders: Are they
different?" *Harvard Business Review, March/April 1992*
70(2) (1992): 26-135. First published May/June 1977,
55(3), 67-76; Zaleznik, Abraham. "Managers and Leaders:
Are They Different?" *Harvard Business Review*, 2004.

38 Peter J., Laurence and Hull, Raymond. *The Peter Principle.*
William Morrow and Company, 1969.

39 Alessandro Pluchino et al. "The Peter principle revisited: A computational study." Physica A: Statistical Mechanics and its Applications, Volume 389, Issue 3, 1 February (2010), Pages 467-472.

40 Løgstrup, Knud Ejler. *The Ethical Demand.* University of Notre Dame Press, 1997.

41 Løgstrup, Knud Ejler (Translation). *Humanisme og kristendom.* Originally published in Heretica 5 (1950): 456-74. Reprinted in Erik Knudsen and Ole Wivel (eds). *Kulturdebat 1944-58.* Copenhagen: Gyldendal, 1958: 280-92.

42 Nyberg, André, Lars Alfredsson, Törres Theorell, Hugo Westerlund, Jussi Vahtera, and Mika Kivimäki. "Managerial Leadership And Ischaemic Heart Disease Among Employees: The Swedish WOLF Study." *Occupational And Environmental Medicine 66* (1) (2009): 51-55.

43 Cranston, Susan, and Scott Keller. "Increasing the 'meaning quotient' of work." *McKinsey Quarterly,* (1) (2013): 48-59.

44 Ladegaard, Yun, Bo Netterstrøm, and Roy Langer. *COPEWORK - COPESTRESS Workplace Study.* Bisbebjerg Hospital, Arbejds- & miljømedicinsk Afdeling, 2012.

45 Lindgren, Astrid. *Emil i Lönneberga.* R&S, 1963.

46 World Economic Forum. *The Future of Jobs Report 2018.* Switzerland: World Economic Forum, 2018.

47 Winick, Stephen. "Einstein's Folklore." Library of Congress, December 2013.

48 World Economic Forum. *The Future of Jobs Report 2018.* Switzerland: World Economic Forum, 2018.

49 Gardner, Howard. *Frames of Mind.* New York: Basic Book Inc., 1983.

50 Cranston, Susan, and Scott Keller. "Increasing the 'meaning quotient' of work." *McKinsey Quarterly*, (1) (2013): 48-59.

51 Voluntās Group (unpublished) www.voluntasgroup.com, 2016.

52 Deloitte. *CFO Insights - Unlocking The Secrets Of Employee Engagement.* Deloitte, 2015.

53 Raymond, Catherine, Marie-France Marin, Anne Hand, Shireen Sindi, Robert-Paul Juster, and Sonia J. Lupien. "Salivary Cortisol Levels and Depressive Symptomatology in Consumers and Nonconsumers of Self-Help Books: A Pilot Study." *Neural Plasticity*, 2015.

54 Greatplacetowork. "Lister," www.greatplacetowork.dk/inspiration/rapporter.

55 CIPD. *Health and Well-being at Work.* CIPD Survey Report, 2018.

56 Gallup. *State of the American Workplace.* Washington: Gallup Inc., 2017.

57 YouGov 2017 in Shelton, Michelle, "Performance Management in the 21st Century," MHR 2018.

58 Gallup. *State of the American Workplace.* Washington: Gallup Inc., 2017.

59 Sisodia, Rajendra, Jagdish Sheth, and David Wolfe. *Firms of Endearment: How World-Class Companies Profit from Passion and Purpose.* Pearson FT Press, 2014.

60 Havas Group. "Meaningful Brands," 2019; Havas Group. "Meaningful Brands," 2017.

61 Cranston, Susan, and Scott Keller. "Increasing the 'meaning quotient' of work." *McKinsey Quarterly*, (1) (2013): 48-59.

62 Deloitte. *CFO Insights - Unlocking The Secrets Of Employee Engagement.* Deloitte, 2015; Bailey, Catherine, and Adrian Madden. "What Makes Work Meaningful — Or Meaningless." *MIT Sloan Management Review. 57* (2016).

63 Voluntās Group (unpublished). www.voluntasgroup.com, 2016-2019.

64 Gallup. *State of the American Workplace.* Washington: Gallup Inc., 2017.

65 Solomon, Robert. "Corporate Roles, Personal Virtues - An Aristotelian Approach to Business Ethics." Cambridge University, Business Ethics Quarterly. Vol. 2, No. 3, (1992).

66 United Nations. "Kyoto Protocol to the United Nations Framework Convention on Climate Change," 1997; United Nations. "United Nations Framework Convention on Climate Change," 1992.

67 Robert Costanza, Maureen Hart, Stephen Posner, and John Talberth. "Beyond GDP: The Need for New Measures of Progress." Bosten University, The Pardee Papers (2009); Kuznets, Simon. National Income 1929–1932. A report to the US Senate, 73rd Congress, 2nd Session. Washington, DC. US Government Printing Office (1934).

68 Mental Health Foundation. "Stress: Are we coping?" London: Mental Health Foundation, May 2018.

69 Willis Towers Watson. *Global Benefits Attitudes Survey.* Willis Towers Watson, 2017.

70 Miller, Lee J., and Wei Lu. "Gen Z Is Set to Outnumber Millennials Within a Year." *Bloomberg*, 20 August 2018.